steve mcalphabet explains ABC² economics

by

Steve McAllister

www.stevemcy.xyz
@SteveMcAlphabet

CONTENTS

PRELUDE

"You do not need to know precisely what is happenging,
or exactly where it is all going.
What you need is to recognize
the possibilities and challanges offered by the present moment,
and to embrace them with courage, faith, and hope."
- Thomas Merton

When I was diagnosed with Attention Deficit Hyperactivity Disorder (without the hyperactivity) at the age of 29, I decided to combine my collected knowledge in psychology and film production to make a documentary about the disorder that was affecting so many people. I interviewed a handful of local professionals that specialized in the field, and had a cameraman follow me around as I rambled on about what it was like to be disordered and how it had been evidenced in my life. When I asked the professionals about what the afflicted could do to help themselves lead a successful life, the most common answer was "structure".

My therapist also gave me a book called *ADD: A Different Perspective* by Thom Hartman. He introduced what he called the "hunter in a farmer's world" theory. The idea is that since humans were initially hunter-gatherers, some of us still identify with that lifestyle and find it challenging to fit into the farming ideologies that have set the standard through the Agricultural and Industrial Revolutions.

It seems that most of the world I live in operates under this agricultural/industrial model, but from my perspective, it creates a lot of waste, in energy, attention, opportunities, and literal garbage. So while I could have just succumbed to my own disorder and done what was required to get with the program, I considered my society's disorder as much more disastrous than my own, and I opted to keep doing my thing, and just amp it up more. To be honest, I've wasted a lot of energy, attention, and opportunities as well, but fortunately, society and I still exist, and both of us still have room for improvement.

Although I initially shirked the structure while creating a new life for myself as I traveled across the country, wrote a few books, songs, stories, and poems, and found other opportunities to excel as a performer and lifestyle stuntman, I have since seen where structure can be helpful. However, while my way of operating in the world has not always been conducive toward supporting the economic structure currently in place, I feel that it would be very wise to reconsider what our economy is actually supposed to do, and develop a structure that will truly help us reach our actual goals.

While our current economic structure is built on a 10,000 year old hierarchical model that is increasing economic inequality, squandering our resources, and damaging the environment, I believe that a more democratic economic structure can be developed considering the technologies now available to us.

The structure I would like to see built is an economic channeling system that can contribute to the continued evolution of human civilization by more greatly empowering people to participate in our development, both personally and collectively.

Since we are now developing a global economy, it is important to base any shared ideology on a multi-cultural paradigm of balance in order to establish an interdependent web of community collaboration and resource-based economics. As you will see, the theory of ABC^2 Economics uses a simple foundation of the four key elements that permeate nearly all human cultures and traditions. By realizing our unity and connection, we can create an economy that works for all.

I have to be honest, I have no idea how ones and zeros make computers work. It boggles my mind to consider how sequences of numbers, letters, and other characters create algoritms, graphics, sounds, and visuals that happen on a computer screen. So my technical jargon throughout the rest of this journey will be limited.

However, I was a poet before I was anything else so, in addition to a more articulate overview of what we're facing and how we face it, I've infused the following pages with some poetic perspectives on what ABC^2 Economics is about and how it can serve us as well.

Granted, the entire theory of ABC^2 Economics is largely a game of “what if?” But that has been a required question for any advance, innovation, improvement, or initiative that humankind has ever experienced. As a matter of fact, the ancient Greek word for money was *nomisma*, which is derived from the verb "to imagine". If we've been able to imagine the civilization we have developed to this point using the money we've created, couldn't we imagine a world in which it works even better?

As such, for any who say this vision is not possible, the next question is, why not?

In his book *The Inevitable: Understanding the 12 Technological Forces That Will Shape Our Future*, Kevin Kelly points out that "Question makers will be seen, properly, as the engines that generate the new fields, new industries, new brands, new possibilities, new continents that our restless species can explore. Questioning is simply more powerful than answering."

So... what if we could do things differently?

ANOTHER WORLD IS OUT THERE

A Tribute to Joseph Campbell

we always start right where we are
to become who we can
in this ordinary land
but another world is out there
to heed the call that beckons us
to abandon all our plans
adventure understands
that another world is out there
when first we refuse the call
can't see a way through it all
if we don't jump, there's no way we can fall
we feel so small
on the word of those
who have blazed the paths before
we can't ignore
that another world is out there
the wisdom of the ages
through our mentors
calls us to explore
because another world is out there
though times seem dark
there is a light that is inside us
let it ignite us
to see another world is out there

our leaders went astray
but there's bliss we can follow
to build a new tomorrow
for the other world that's out there
crossing that first threshold
taking one step at a time
as we finally cross the line
toward the other world that's out there
we are tested, we are bested
we make enemies and friends
we will not be this way again
move toward the other world that's out there
your life is painted on the walls of your inmost cave
yours is the only soul you can save
you fear life more than you fear the grave
but you must be brave
the only thing that's in our way is our way
as we replay
the memories that we swear
create our lives in the image of our ordeals
we will reveal
that another world is out there
we are the heroes we've been waiting on to
manifest our dreams
however bad things seem
another world is out there
we cannot wait for others
to make the journey for us
embrace apotheosis
to see the other world it's out there
when opportunity presents itself
will you seize the sword?

realize the reward
is that another world is out there
be resurrected in the image of all possibilities
make no apologies
for seeing that another world is out there
the road back home is littered with broken plans
and shattered dreams
yet it forks and it twists and it blossoms
with wide-eyed strategies and schemes
to remind us that when life flows
gratitude makes it stream
or so it seems
so a toast to the elixir of our evolution
may we see solutions
in the other world that's out there
though illusions make it seem we can't achieve it
if we believe it
another world is out there
the cave you fear to enter
holds the treasure that you seek
there's no time to be meek
for another world is out there
the universe is calling us to complete
feel it in our heart beats
that another world is out there

OVERVIEW

"You never change things
by fighting against the existing reality.
To change something,
build a new model that makes the old model obsolete."
- Buckminster Fuller

As its greatest proponents will often tell you, America supports capitalism, and the capitalism we believe in is supported by the "free market". If we're going to use the market to its fullest potential, before moving forward, we should at least glean what we can from its greatest advocates. In *Capitalism and Freedom*, Milton Friedman stated that the role of the market, "is that it permits unanimity without conformity; that it is a system of effectively proportional representation."

So it would serve us well to figure out how our participation in the market can create a more proportionally represented financial flow. To do that, we're going to need to understand the role of money in all of this activity we call "wealth".

The big challenge we face under the economic system we feel beholden to is that it twists the definition of money, turning it from a tool that people should be able to use so that the economy can flow into a commodity people hoard so they can see their egos grow. And while capitalism may work just fine in the sandbox of the "free market", where children build their castles and draw their boundaries, in the greater playground of the real world, it's often just a screwed up little game for bullies who steal your freedom and force you to buy it back from them. Nevertheless, if we recognize the game for what it really is, and if we realize how much power we actually have, the playground is going to be a much happier place.

After all, "Money is only a tool," as Ayn Rand reminds us in *Atlas Shruggea*. "It will take you wherever you wish, but it will not replace you as the driver."

Now, it is also said that America supports democracy, but if we seek to have a market that actually supports democracy and works for the entirety of the population, we should let the population drive it.

Unfortunately, as Dr. Martin Luther King pointed out before he was assassinated, "Capitalism does not permit an even flow of economic resources. With this system, a small, privileged few are rich beyond conscience, and almost all others are doomed to be poor at some level. That's the way the system works. And since we know that the system will not change the rules, we are going to have to change the system."

It is important to understand that the economy we serve now - the currencies and organizations that promote them - is of human creation. Every cent, every euro, every yen, every bitcoin, and every other unit of finance was created by the human imagination. They are only reality because we believe them to be.

Every job that we have manifested in civilization is also a human creation. Although we have been taught to value them more than most anything else in the world, several of them are extremely non-essential for our existence or fulfillment. Especially in an economy based on financial speculation (bullshit) and rampant consumerism (garbage), many of the jobs we're coerced to do are actually wasteful and, in the big picture, destructive.

Science fiction author Arthur C. Clarke once said, "The goal of the future is full unemployment, so we can play," and Wendell Berry agreed unemployment was, "without exaggeration... the present national ambition of the United States. People live for quitting time, for weekends, for vacations, and for retirement; moreover, this ambition seems to be classless, as true in the executive suites as on the assembly lines. One works not because the work is necessary, valuable, useful to a desirable end, or because one loves to do it, but only to be able to quit - a condition that a saner time would regard as infernal, a condemnation."

As such, our goals should be better applied toward virtuous intentions and serving our common needs instead of serving only the greed of a few. Now, obviously, much work is actually fulfilling, and many people find great purpose in the services and craftsmanship they offer. However, many more are demanded to toil through the majority of their time doing tasks that do not cultivate joy, but only serve to create profits for people who don't actually do the work while creating unnecessary waste of both natural resources and human potential.

"True progress begins with something no knowledge economy can produce: wisdom about what it means to live well," writes Rutger Bregman in *Utopia for Realists: How We Can Build the Ideal World*. "We have to do what great thinkers like John Stuart Mill, Bertrand Russell, and John Maynard Keynes were already advocating 100 years ago: to 'value ends above means and prefer the good to the useful.' We have to direct our minds to the future. To stop consuming our own discontent through polls and the relentlessly bad news media. To consider alternatives and form new collectives. To transcend this confining zeitgeist and recognize our shared idealism."

If the history of technological evolution and innovation has taught us anything, it is that we can continue to improve the system, but we must create better goals. Although many of our technologies have been used to propagate the separation that has created many of the problems now facing humanity, other tools have also given us the ability to transcend the problems we've created and evolve into an improved economy.

Granted, for those with eyes to see, we cannot continue to myopically regard everything as merely "capital" and trust that capitalism will save the day. Nor can we rely on fully embracing the tenets of communism or socialism any more than we can look forward to reverting to feudalism. Although we may not yet know the name of the economic construct that will deliver us from our addiction to imbalance, we know that something has to change.

"It is never possible to know in advance what may or may not occur," says Gar Alperovitz in *What Then Must We Do?: Straight Talk about the Next American Revolution*. "Nonetheless, such a time is a time when it is also our responsibility to begin to consider the fundamental question of how a 'next system' might and should be organized, a time to begin to explore new ways to achieve the great American values that can no longer be achieved by the dying system."

Every task we create is used to reach certain goals, and each goal is a human creation. We are now at a time in human history where actual democratic action is more possible than ever before, but we must reconsider the goals we have for our economy and act accordingly. Historically, many goals have been hijacked to merely increase financial development for the wealthy. Our focus has been guided toward the measurement of value and vain competitions, which has enabled the social disease that is greed to encourage hoarding and sociopathy. Moving forward, we would be wise to focus our energies on goals that would actually develop the sustainability, resilience, and quality of life the majority of us truly desire.

For quite a while, and especially since the dawn of capitalism, the accumulation of money seems to have become one of our key goals. So instead of regarding money for the currency that it is, it has thrown us off kilter by becoming the goal in itself.

"It's critical to understand the definition of the word 'currency'," explains Bernard A. Lietaer in *Rethinking Money: How New Currencies Turn Scarcity into Prosperity*. "So for me currency is information between a buyer and a seller... Money is not valuable at all, but money allows you to buy things, which are valuable. This distinction should be understood. And it's not generally known or appreciated by most people."

Unfortunately, instead of understanding money better and empowering it to flow as it should, we have largely become consumed with the competition for it. Although we often herald money as the bringer of convenience and prosperity, due to our methods of venerating those who have the most unhealthy cravings for it, money has somehow come to represent the scarcity and lack it was supposed to overcome.

"The strangest of all the doctrines of the cult of competition," explains Wendell Berry in *What Are People For?*, "in which admittedly there must be losers as well as winners, is that the result of competition is inevitably good for everybody, that altruistic ends may be met by a system without altruistic motives or altruistic means."

Historically, violence, hierarchy, patriarchy, and competition have dominated the story humanity tells itself. This has indeed been an immature understanding of who we actually are and a devastating limitation on our potential. As humanity continues to evolve and our civilization changes, we are realizing the sheer folly behind many of these antiquated programs, and many are awakening to their power to tell the story of abundance, collaboration, equality, and connection that our technologies and innovations have empowered.

As Geoffrey West explains in *Scale: The Universal Laws of Growth, Innovation, Sustainability, and the Pace of Life in Organisms, Cities, Economies, and Companies*, "We need to understand how the dynamics of innovation, technological advances, urbanization, financial markets, social networks, and population dynamics are interconnected and how their evolving interrelationships fuel growth and societal change - and, as manifestations of human endeavors, how they are all integrated into a holistic interacting systemic framework . . . and whether such a dynamically evolving system is ultimately sustainable."

Moving forward into the economy we seek, we would be wise to look at the natural economy of the planet we're on and recognize how it is distributive and regenerative by design, unlike the divisive and degenerative nature of our man-made economic model of rewarding the insanity of relentless competition at all costs. If we want to build a model of sustainability, Mother Nature has done an extraordinary job of creating a number of really helpful examples.

"Systems biologists find that the healthy functioning of any living system depends on collaboration," says David Korten in *Change The Story, Change The Future: A Living Economy For A Living Earth*. "Most all living organisms exist, thrive, and co-evolve only within living communities engaged in a continuous synergistic sharing and exchange that from a big-picture perspective is fundamentally cooperative."

If we are to make an economic system sustainably, it must be based on collaboration, in which prosperity can be shared throughout the populace, instead of continuing to base it on competition to ensure that only the most ruthless, selfish, and uncaring thrive. In order for a currency to be fully functional, whether that currency be the Federal Reserve Note or any of the other national, complementary, or digital currencies being developed, it must properly distribute the energy that the currency represents and help it to circulate. If money is the lifeblood of a society, if it does not circulate properly, as we have seen, disease sets in.

"An economy that is distributive by design," says Kate Raworth in *Doughnut Economics*, "is one whose dynamics tend to disperse and circulate value as it is created, rather than concentrating it in ever-fewer hands. An economy that is regenerative by design is one in which people become full participants in regenerating Earth's life-giving cycles so that we thrive within planetary boundaries."

And full participation is what we truly seek. Fully ensconced in the Information Revolution, where nannies have been replaced by smartphones and tablets, we are becoming a generation of clicking, swiping, life-hacking, skill-gathering, open-minded, open-sourced explorers of virtual reality on a never-ending inquiry into what's possible. As Kevin Kelly points out in *The Inevitable: Understanding the 12 Technological Forces That Will Shape Our Future*, "In the coming 30 years, anything that is not intensely interactive will be considered broken."

By changing the goals of our economy, we can change our story. According to Charles Eisenstein, we have been playing out the "Story of Separation", and the "Story of Sacred Money and Markets", according to David Korten. Our current story has reduced our identity to consumers as a way of commoditizing every natural resource on the planet, including our time, talent, relationships, and passions. This has been done in order to make as much money as possible for a very small, self-serving, and short-sighted percentile of the population. If we can eliminate, or at least deescalate, competitive, predatory, and destructive behavior, we can tell a new story: one that celebrates the greater abundance of being citizens in a natural, balanced economy. We can move toward telling what Eisenstein calls the "Story of Interbeing" and what Korten calls the "Story of a Living Earth", but we must realize the power we have to tell a new story and participate in the new revolution.

"The level of transformation required now is inconceivable without a change of consciousness and a new planetary culture," says Daniel Pinchbeck in *How Soon is Now: From Personal Initiation to*

Global Transformation. "But we may be on the cusp of a wisdom revolution - and it could happen quickly. As the futurist Peter Russell points out, revolutions in human culture unfold in exponentially shorter time frames. The Agricultural Revolution started eight to ten thousand years ago, leading to the development of a surplus which was necessary for the growth of cities, and a complex, differentiated social system. The Industrial Revolution took around five hundred years, with its roots going back to the Middle Ages. The Information Revolution - the linking of the planetary community together through networks of data and communication - has happened within a half-century or so."

Russell goes on to elaborate on what he calls the Wisdom Revolution by pointing out the exponential growth of human information technologies and how it is rapidly moving us toward a time "when all human knowledge will be instantly available to anyone on the planet, in any medium." Because we are all connected to this "emerging global mind," we are approaching "a qualitative shift, first, from information to knowledge and then from knowledge to wisdom."

Having grown through the Agrarian, Agricultural, Industrial, and Information Revolutions, we are now poised to enter the Revolution of Wisdom by realizing ourselves as more than any limited social roles we've previously been assigned, but as whole beings capable of fully participating in the world around us as equal contributors. Perched on the divide between

Renaissance and Dark Age, it would seem we have two choices. We can open to all facets of our being and embrace a better world for all. Or we can shrink from our greatness and allow the most selfish among us to continue telling the story of flagrant consumption, indebtedness, and destruction. (Actually, other than American politics, there's just about always more than two choices, usually many more.)

"Until now," Pinchbeck points out, "our focus has been technological progress, not social innovation. Our society has been focused on making things that make profit, not on reinventing our social system to support the greatest level of happiness, self-knowledge and freedom for all. What would happen if we changed our focus?"

The revolution we seek need not be like the violent revolutions we have seen in the past, but more of a realization, or as Pinchbeck calls it, "a peaceful revolution - a gentle superseding of the current political-economic system, not an explosive insurrection against it. We need a revolution that is, at the same time, evolution and revelation."

Indeed, it may seem like a daunting task to completely reinvent the economy. As Paul Mason writes in *Postcapitalism: A Guide To Our Future*, "Today we have to relearn to do positive things, to build alternatives within the system; to use governmental power in a radical and disruptive way; and to focus all our actions towards the transition path - not the piecemeal defense of random elements of the old system."

Just as we are realizing the necessity to shift our way of doing things, new technologies are emerging to empower us to make the changes we seek. With the launch of bitcoin, the first well-known cryptocurrency, came the infrastructure of blockchain, a decentralized, digital peer-to-peer platform for tracking exchanges of value. While none of the cryptocurrencies have the distinction of being partially represented by actual material, like the less than 10% of Federal Reserve Notes that are actually cash, similarly to how the other 90% of what we consider legal tender, as digital entities, they still seem to have the capacity to be used as money.

As Kate Raworth explains in *Doughnut Economics*, blockchain's name "derives from the blocks of data - each one a snapshot of all transactions that have just been made in the network - which are linked together to create a chain of data blocks, adding up to a minute-by-minute record of the network's activity. And since that record is stored on every computer in the network, it acts as a public ledger that cannot be altered, corrupted or deleted, making it a highly secure digital backbone for the future of e-commerce and transparent governance."

Realizing how inefficient many institutions have become in an age where children have more daily access to digital technology than their parents even dreamed of, the idea of blockchain is to replace these "institutions with technology that can do the job better and empowers individuals," writes Alan T. Norman in *Blockchain Technology*

Explainea. "If you could create a way for strangers to trust one another without needing a bank or a government as an intermediary, you'd tackle one of society's biggest bottlenecks."

But it won't just be bitcoin and the US dollar that will be used to advance our economy. Although they have both proven that they can exist and thrive as virtual currencies with no inherent value, they have also paved the way for other virtual currencies to find their way into the market. In *The Business Blockchain: Promise, Practice, and Application of the Next Internet Technology*, William Mougayar estimates that dozens of commonly used, global virtual currencies will contribute 5 trillion dollars to the economy and represent 5% of the world's 100 trillion dollar economy in 2025.

Many, like Don Tapscott, author of *Blockchain Revolution: How the Technology Behind Bitcoin Is Changing Money, Business and the World,* believe that "blockchain technology could be an important tool for protecting and preserving humanity and the rights of every human being, a means of communicating the truth, distributing prosperity, and — as the network rejects the fraudulent transactions — of rejecting those early cancerous cells from a society that can grow into the unthinkable."

Although blockchain may very well be a pivotal piece to the puzzle of how we recreate our economy, it is important to realize that, like money itself, it is only a tool. What matters is not so much what we use, but why and how we use it.

The vision for ABC^2 Economics is that it will allow people to direct the flow of their currency to fluidly support the Artistry of life. It is done through the Business of good service, by practicing responsible Citizenry, and creating a more sustainable Community with a higher quality of life. Artistry. Business. Citizenry. Community. These are the why's and how's of ABC^2 Economics.

It is estimated that 91.5% of the planet's money supply is now digital, and no longer cash and coin as in previous generations. What if we were to develop an algorithm to channel digital monies used in transactions into portfolios based on preset directives? Theoretically, every transaction should address the costs of the Artistry and Business expenses required, as well as the Citizenry of investing in the infrastructure that allows the transaction to happen, while also supporting the surrounding Community by empowering charitable endeavors and social profit organizations.

As you'll read in the coming pages, in order to put ABC^2 Economics into practice, people should be able to create their own "webmap". A webmap will empower people to create an online profile and participate in the market as artists and people of business. It would also allow them to choose which governmental endeavors, non-profit organizations, and other charities they want to support, making them less reliant on the wastefulness of bureaucracy and more resilient in creating the kind of world we want to live in.

To find our balance with the natural world and become people of the new Renaissance, we need to move into the Revolution of Wisdom and pay attention to what Mother Nature has been doing for the last several eons. It will serve us well to realize the alignment between the balanced elements of the natural world - water, air, earth, and fire - and the elements of human individuals - heart, mind, body, and spirit. Through this realization, we can better recognize the societal elements of Artistry, Business, Citizenry, and Community as ABC^2 Economics can help us find our balance as both individuals and a collective.

Individually, ABC^2 Economics is designed to draw our attention toward our emotional, mental, physical, and spiritual health. It is also designed to bring structure to the collective, helping us to distribute the energy we use wisely among participating members in order to develop a healthier economic flow than the childish winner-take-all scenario that has so often hindered true economic development in the past, and continues to do so in the present. Through our community efforts, we can eliminate the suffering caused by our activities and endeavors, past, present, and future.

In his 1996 report for the Federal Reserve Bank, "Money is Memory", Naravana Kocherlakota noted that, "Since the dawn of its use, money has been used to account for things, a way to remember who did what, who contributed what, who used what, and who used whom." Basically, after all of the fuss that we make about money, as

Kocherlakota went on, "if we account for the fact that money itself is useless, monetary allocations are merely large interlocking networks of gifts."

While this may stand in contrast to the proponents of commerce and their absolute adherence to the mystical "free market" and tit-for-tat necessities it seems to require, the fact that it is described as "free" regards even the market itself as some sort of sacred gift. For those fortunate enough to find a place in the market where they can do what they love as purposeful service to the world, the joy of the economy isn't the money they make, but the gifts they've been given and get to share. However, a great many people have to work very, very hard to participate in the "free" market without feeling like a slave to it.

Would that we could remember the gift that life is and base our economy on that principle instead of viewing life as debt. Although a relatively small portion of the population is insecure enough to have hoarded more than their necessary share of the wealth humanity has created, their insatiable hunger for more has drawn a large portion of that wealth to them. Imagine if the rest of us were to use what's left to create a system based on the concept of the gift in order to create an economy of true wealth, beyond the numbers we use to represent it.

"In the beginning was the Gift," says Charles Eisenstein in *Sacred Economics*. "We are born helpless infants, creatures of pure need with little resource to give, yet we are fed, we are protected, we are clothed and held and soothed, without having done anything to deserve it, without offering anything in exchange. This experience, common to everyone who has made it past childhood, informs some of our deepest spiritual intuitions. Our lives are given us: therefore, our default state is gratitude."

In our technologically advanced modern society, for the first time in known human history, we stand poised to develop an economy that can work for everyone and truly represent democracy. This is where ABC² Economics seeks to be of assistance.

THE CHALLENGE BEFORE US

from my perspective, it would seem
that before us we have a challenge
we have created an economy
that isn't very balanced
largely because finance
has become the go-to industry
but we have barely scratched the surface
of our true ability
to use this tool with more intent
than to merely profit, gain, and grow
the size of our carbon footprint
and the sizes of our egos
the way things have been done before
have largely been based on hierarchy
but the way in which we're moving now
is much more about democracy
many of us have been very well trained
to serve the people at the top
but many more have realized
it's time for this to stop
it seems as if we've reached a point
where there could be some tipping
and we can give power to the people
if we can do some more equipping
of understanding who we really are
and just what we can do

to flip the hierarchy
and create the world anew
so let's start it out, we all have hearts
and we struggle with emotions
but they make us feel alive
and they offer us the notion
that the water in our tears
is the water that sustains us
and like tides and ebbs, rivers and streams
the flow does much to change us
and how we deal with the waves we feel
the process of that catharsis
is ultimately up to us
and if we live our lives as artists
we create our moments
and listen to our minds
we choose the voices to ignore
and the ones that help us find
the way to higher purpose
and actions that have meaning
when we can feel of service
and ideas start their streaming
just as water becomes a cloud
our emotions become ideas
and when that light bulb goes off
usually our tendency is
to start another business
to create another stream
of revenue to rise to the challenge
to manifest our dream
for generations, it has been enough
to engage with things we create and sell

we're the only species to have art or markets
and we think it's pretty swell
but as we grow in knowledge
hopefully, we also grow in wisdom
and as we continue to evolve
we have to make new decisions
humans are a complex lot
we are more than just thoughts and emotions
we also have these bodies
like land emerged from oceans
the water that flows through us
renders blood and flesh and bone
inhabiting these earth suits
our minds and hearts have found a home
living in our bodies we experience the world
and matter becomes what matters
as reality unfurls
because we're different than other critters
we make weapons, tools, and music
we often get caught up in our own power
and sometimes we abuse it
some of us don't even consider ourselves
as being part of nature
and this ignorant entitlement
creates some really bad behavior
when we emerge from this planet
we claim it as our birthright
then we strip it, mine it, and suck it dry
never realizing that it's finite
but if we can get back to reality
remember we're beasts and realize we are burdens
our species is called *homo sapiens*
and that's supposed to mean wise person

now whoever came up with that one
was feeling pretty hopeful
because it seems our foolish ways
have the planet in a chokehold
now, it's not all our faults
because we've been trained to be consumers
but we gotta wake up and implement wisdom
if we want our species to have a future
we can still be artists and we can still have business
but we've got to use some discipline
we've got to be more than programmed consumers
we've got to rise up and be citizens
so if you want to change the world
this is your opportunity
to realize we are all part of the all
we are all one big global community

WHY WE NEED TO REDEVELOP THE ECONOMY

"We do not need to have a picture of what a true world would be like in order to feel that there is something radically wrong with the world that exists."
—John Holloway, *Change the World Without Taking Power: The Meaning of Revolution Today*

Albert Einstein is often quoted as saying, "If I had an hour to solve a problem, I'd spend 55 minutes thinking about the problem and 5 minutes thinking about solutions." There is much wisdom in clarifying a problem before starting to work on the solution so let's at least start by looking at the problems of our current economic system before we look to change it.

- We live in a time of record economic inequality and instability due to our adherence to a debt-based, industrial finance model. This model has been bolstered by the U.S. Supreme Court's *Citizens United* decision, which gives corporations the same rights as human beings. This has dramatically drawn political power from the true citizenry of the people and given it to financial institutions.

- Our current economic model is based on the principle of rewarding avarice, separation, violence, and dishonesty instead of the virtues of cooperation, community, harmony, and trust that we truly seek.
- The continued application of trickle down economics has served to enable a small minority of the population to garner political control, leaving the rest of the population feeling disenfranchised, divided, powerless, and in a constant state of dread over financial instability.
- While a republic was sufficient for 1776, the oligarchy of 2021 is not what the founding fathers envisioned. We need to move toward a truer democracy and an even more perfect union.
- Many of our forefathers feared competition among warring political factions. As they feared, these factions have turned the U.S. government into a wasteful cesspool of corruption and money laundering that is incapable of meeting the needs of the people.
- Although the US dollar had been pegged as the global currency for thirty years, President Richard Nixon released the Federal Reserve Note from the gold standard in 1971. Money has not had comparable material value or accountability since, creating an economic system based

on a global fiat currency with no intrinsic value.

- In addition to the world's many nationally based fiat currencies, the development of crypto-currencies has initiated an economy replete with new possibilities for consumption; however, it has not offered a clear strategy on how to create an actual sustainable economy.
- The economy of consumption is spurred on by short-term profiteering and deluded thinking that there could be endless fossil fuels and crude materials on a finite planet. The abuse of our nature has created extreme environmental negativities, such as deforestation, pollution, species extinction, climate change, and wastefulness.
- Americans were once considered "citizens" who excelled in cultural developments and community. Now, as our identities have been transformed into "consumers", we are suffering from mental and physical diseases, record violence, and social dysfunction. The "land of the free" now has the highest incarceration rate of any country on the planet, per capita and as a total population.
- The traditional economic systems of capitalism, communism, and socialism are still enmeshed in authoritarianism; hence, they are incapable of truly empowering people. We still lack a robust economy in

which people are not subjugated to having their money taken from them before they even get it and forced to support endeavors that do not work in their best interests.

In the development of our mainstream economy, we have made a number of mistakes. We're human, so mistakes are just part of the learning process, but our humanity also affords us the ability to learn from our mistakes and grow from them rather than continuing to repeat them. So let's be honest about the system we've been encouraged to blindly protect and uphold, and open up to the possibility that, as with every other advancement humanity has achieved, something better is possible.

As Nobel prize-winning economist Joseph Stiglitz says in *People, Power, and Profits: Progressive Capitalism for an Age of Discontent*. "We thought unfettered markets were the solution to every economic problem; we thought finance and globalization and advances in technology would, on their own, bring prosperity to all. We thought that markets were, on their own, always competitive - and so we didn't understand the dangers of market power. We thought the blind pursuit of profits would lead to societal well-being. We got our politics wrong: too many thought that just having elections was all that democracy was about... we got our values wrong. We forgot that the economy is supposed to serve our citizens, not the other way around."

Unfortunately, finance has come to overtake all other industries as the key economic driver in

America. Even though it only represents about 7% of our economy and creates only 4% of the jobs, according to Rana Foroohar in *Makers and Takers: The Rise of Finance and the Fall of American Business*, it takes about 25% of corporate profits.

Yet although the United States could brag about having three times the financial assets of the next three richest countries combined in 2015, it did nothing to improve economic growth for the majority of Americans, not even those who put in the labor upon which speculations were made and through which the game of finance was made possible. Instead, it has actually slowed things down for the average citizen since the economic energy they create is immediately absorbed into the accounts of those who discuss it over phone calls and golf games.

"Whatever the cause, the United States is privately rich but socially poor," says Jeffrey D. Sachs, *The Price Of Civilization: Reawakening American Virtue And Prosperity*. "It caters to the pursuit of wealth but pays scant attention to those left behind. And though American culture emphasizes individualism and the pursuit of individual wealth perhaps more than any other society, that focus does not lead to greater happiness."

As Nobel Prize-winning economist Angus Deaton and his colleague Daniel Kahneman discovered through their research at the Center for Health and Well-Being at Princeton University, money actually can buy happiness, but only to a certain point. According to the peer-reviewed study, having the ability to provide for all of your needs and feasibly achieve self actualization costs about 75,000$ a year. Money made beyond that point appears to become relatively superfluous and does not seem to increase enjoyment of day-to-day experiences. Our challenge is that we've somehow bought into the idea that accumulating as much as possible is the highest of virtues, and since we are somewhat forced, or at least subconsciously coerced, to exert more energy than necessary to reach goals we intrinsically know do not work in our own best interests, we have a number of emotional issues and some true struggles with achieving happiness.

And although we're led to believe that having fifty different varieties of Oreo cookies and a few dozen different types of toothpaste should provide us with the purposeful choices that make life worth living, many of us feel that the amount of work we have to do in order to make those choices isn't worth it. Many of us feel, and rightfully so, that we're being taken advantage of.

"For three decades after World War II," Robert B. Reich reminds us in *Saving Capitalism: For the Many, Not the Few.* "America created the largest middle class the world had ever seen. During those years the earnings of the typical American worker doubled, just as the size of the American economy doubled. Over the last thirty years, by contrast, the size of the economy doubled again but the earnings of the typical American went nowhere. Then, CEOs of large corporations earned an average of about twenty times the pay of their typical worker. Now they get substantially over two hundred times. In those years, the richest 1 percent of Americans took home 9 to 10 percent of total income; today the top 1 percent gets more than 20 percent."

Although many tried to dismiss the Occupy movement that started on Wall Street as a rebellious antic caused by economic angst, their cries did not go unheard. Unfortunately, we have yet to find an adequate solution to deal with the challenges that face us and the system that has enslaved us. Yet looking at the past may give us some clearer insight as to how to progress into the future.

"The parallel between ancient Rome and the present day is striking," says Charles Eisenstein in *Sacred Economics*. "Now as then, wealth is increasingly concentrated in the hands of the few. Now as then, people must go into lifelong debt that they can never pay off just to have access to the necessities of life. Then it was through access to land; today it is through access to money. The slaves, serfs, and tenants gave a lifetime of labor to the enrichment of the landowners; today the proceeds of our labor go to the owners of money."

When slavery, the forced servitude we've become familiar with through films like *Amistad*, *12 Years a Slave*, and *Django Unchained*, was practiced in America, the slaveowners would still provide food and housing for the slaves, as meager as it may have been. In the capitalism so many are currently enslaved by, servants are largely required to work for the owners of capital in order to pay the owners of capital for food and housing, as well as the other necessities of life. Unfortunately, the servants are having to work longer and harder to appease the insatiable appetites of the owners of capital.

"Over the past half-century or so," says Richard Florida in *The Great Reset*, "the amount of money the average American family spends on housing and cars has skyrocketed. From 1950 to the mid-1980s, the amount allotted for housing and cars doubled from 22 percent to 44 percent of its budget. (At the same time, the amount the average American family had to devote to health care rose threefold, from 5.2 percent in the late 1950s to 14.8 percent by the year 2000.) A generation ago, all of life's basic necessities - housing, transportation, health insurance, education, and taxes - accounted for 54 percent of the average family's income; today, they account for 75 percent of it."

It would seem that the economic system we've been following somehow thrives on instability, including the insecurity of the consumers and servants who enable it. As so many in the populace teeter precariously between employment and homelessness, those who've realized the rules to the game of economics are able to make huge sums of money on the misery created through the systems' unquestionable shortcomings.

"Our identification of what is wrong is straightforward," Hyman Minsky wrote in *Stabilizing An Unstable Economy*. "Since the mid-

1960s, the economy has been characterized by turbulence in the form of financial instability, inflation, and rising unemployment, along with a sharp slowdown in the pace at which living standards improve. This turbulence stands in sharp contrast to the tranquility and progress that ruled in the prior twenty years. The conclusion of the analytical argument is that turbulence - especially financial instability - is normal in a capitalist economy; the tranquil era between 1946 and 1966 was an anomaly."

Indeed, according to the study "Economics and Happiness: Framing the Analysis" by Luigino Bruni and Pier Luigi Porta, America seems to have hit its peak happiness levels in 1956. Throughout this period, Americans enjoyed a higher rate of economic equality, greater social mobility and spending power, lower crime, and a GI Bill that gave an education to 7.8 million veterans who needed a way to deal with what they had experienced in battle. And although it allowed for a surge in real estate as suburbia spread throughout the land, the stability enjoyed during this time, which built upon what many would consider the socialist notions of the New Deal, would not last as the speculation of finance, the inordinate amount of bullshit required to manufacture instability through the ideology of scarcity, came to dominate our economic system.

Since then, we've come to fully embrace the notions of planned obsolescence, which requires us to make products that don't last and need to be replaced in order to keep the economy moving, and fractional reserve banking, where banks can seemingly create money out of thin air by borrowing against money that doesn't exist. The insanity of our system is that, while it seems to flourish on the idea of scarcity, it doesn't recognize it in the real world.

"The problem is," as Paul Mason states in *Postcapitalism: A Guide To Our Future*, "mainstream economics does not understand its own limitations."

With finance as the economic driver, our economy must feed on every resource available to us in order to turn them into units of currency, largely represented by digital dollars with no intrinsic value. So even though it looks impressive to the simple minds that are impressed by big numbers as the GDP grows, the reality is that we are sacrificing every ounce of the ancient sunlight that is oil, every oxygen-providing tree, every drop of life-giving water, and every calorie of human energy in order to create units of light and information that we can gather together for those who have no dirt under their fingernails. We must rethink the true goals of economic growth.

"While exponential growth" says Geoffrey West in *Scale: The Universal Laws of Growth, Innovation, Sustainability, and the Pace of Life in Organisms, Cities, Economies, and Companies*, "is a remarkable manifestation of our extraordinary accomplishments as a species, built into it are the potential seeds of our demise and the portent of big troubles just around the next corner."

Although there are some that still deny that all of the activity of drilling, burning, melting, and building we've done as a species has had any effect on the environment, most thinking people are coming around to realizing that the majority of scientists who claim that climate change is something to be concerned about are probably more trustworthy than the oil magnates who say it isn't. And since many people have concluded that the pollution we put into the environment does, in fact, have repercussions, we are realizing that the endless economic growth sold to us by those who are reaping the greatest benefits of it may not be the economic goal we should be striving for.

"Mainstream economics views endless economic growth as a must," says Kate Raworth in *Doughnut Economics*, "but nothing in nature grows forever, and the attempt to buck that trend is raising tough questions in high-income but low-growth countries. It may not be hard to give up having GDP growth as an economic goal, but it is going to be far harder to overcome our addiction to it. Today we have economies that need to grow, whether or not they make us thrive; what we need are economies that make us thrive, whether or not they grow. That radical flip in perspective invites us to become agnostic about growth and to explore how economies that are currently financially, politically and socially addicted to growth could learn to live with or without it."

Considering how much of our time and energy is spent in the pursuit of goals we do not actually seek, we need to reconsider how much growth we actually need. Forcing more people to go to unnecessary jobs to revel in bullshit or just to make more garbage may make the economy grow, but it also increases traffic and pollution, and increases the time we have to spend in it.

"Even if we could grow our way out of the crisis and delay the inevitable and painful reconciliation of virtual and real wealth," Herman E. Daly points out in *For the Common Good: Redirecting the economy toward community, the environment, and a sustainable future*, "there is the question of whether this would be a wise thing to do. Marginal costs of additional growth in rich countries, such as global warming, biodiversity loss and roadways choked with cars, now likely exceed marginal benefits of a little extra consumption. The end result is that promoting further economic growth makes us poorer, not richer."

Unfortunately, there is a class of people we have come to revere as "leadership" that is obsessed with growing numbers to the detriment of everything else. Although real people may suffer through terrible ordeals like car accidents, divorces, fires, health problems, natural catastrophes, and public shootings, there are some who merely revel in the fact that all of these things contribute to the rise of the GDP number.

"We have an economic system that fetishizes GDP growth above all else, regardless of the human or ecological consequences," says Naomi Klein in *This Changes Everything: Capitalism vs. The Climate*, "while failing to place value on those things that most of us cherish above all—a decent standard of living, a measure of future security, and our relationships with one another."

What we fail to understand is how our obsession with this number, and our addiction to the drug of "more" has adverse effects not only on the world around us, but on our very souls. Although we may have lessons of morality and ethics shared with us through our movies, religions, storybooks, and fairy tales, teaching us to be humble, caring, and sharing, our lifestyle, and the advertising propaganda that fuels it, tells us to get all we can and consume as much as we want. Few of us recognize this disparity nor the ramifications of our gluttonous habits.

"Human activity is putting unprecedented stress on Earth's life-giving systems," says Kate Raworth in *Doughnut Economics*. "Global average temperature has already risen by 0.8 degrees Celsius, and we are on track for an increase of almost 4 degrees Celsius by 2100, threatening a scale and intensity of floods, droughts, storms and sea-level rise that humanity has never before witnessed. Around 40 percent of the world's agricultural land is now seriously degraded, and by 2025 two out of three people worldwide will live in water-stressed regions. Meanwhile over 80 percent of the world's fisheries are fully or over-exploited and a refuse truck's worth of plastic is dumped into the ocean every minute: at this rate, by 2050, there will be more plastic than fish in the sea."

Granted, plastic is an amazing material. Drawn from ancient sunlight, plastic will last longer than most any other human creation, with some it lasting for several hundred years before breaking down and rejoining the natural cycle of life. However, the idea to make disposable products out of such a long-lasting material was sheer idiocy.

Nevertheless, with the short-sighted goals of the current economic system, it raises the GDP, and we have yet to find a better use for these resources than producing more garbage. The downside is that by using the finite resource that is oil to make garbage, just as we do with so many of our other natural resources, we are selling off our futures for the sake of profits that most of us will never actually enjoy. Will we still seek to appease the capitalists when the oil runs out?

"There is no economic imperative that will condemn us to deplete our vital resource base," Jeffrey D. Sachs reminds us in *Common Wealth: Economics for a Crowded Planet*, "but neither is there an invisible hand that will prevent us from doing so."

Although it is often seen as the guiding light in our journey of endless growth, there is not enough reliable information available to truly confirm that the invisible hand Adam Smith mentioned only three times in his writings isn't just as capable of flipping us off as it is to enable the mental illness we've come to embrace.

Along with that mental illness comes the additional diagnosis of belief in a supernatural free market, where the machines of our kingdoms and corporations can ravage the commons that belong to our collective species and the other inhabitants of this planet in order to turn them into money and never have to pay any reparations or provide any regenerative activity by which the damages and injuries related to their activity can be repaired and healed. The religion of the "free market" and its invisible hand should be separated from the state along with every other church.

For although its adherents declare capitalism to be the best economic system ever, even its greatest proponents had issues with it. For instance, even though John Maynard Keynes, known as the father of modern economics, felt that capitalism was the best system to achieve a civilized economic society, he also recognized that its failure to provide for full employment and the inequitable distribution of wealth and incomes were major faults. He also recognized that its fallibilities would one day bring its demise.

"When the accumulation of wealth is no longer of high social importance, there will be great changes in the code of morals," Keynes wrote in *Economic Possibilities for Our Grandchildren*. "We shall be able to rid ourselves of many of the pseudo-moral principles which have hag-ridden us for two hundred years, by which we have exalted some of the most distasteful of human qualities into the position of the highest virtues. We shall be able to afford to dare to assess the money-motive at its true value. The love of money as a possession — as distinguished from the love of money as a means to the enjoyments and realities of life — will be recognized for what it is, a somewhat disgusting morbidity, one of those semi-criminal, semi-pathological propensities which one hands over with a shudder to the specialists in mental disease."

Unfortunately, the accumulation of wealth did not fall by the wayside as Keynes had hoped. Instead, it has become the most important driver of our economy, so much so that although the system does still seem to work for those with a love of money as a possession, it is not doing enough to actually provide for the well-being of the populace.

As Noam Chomsky stated in an interview with David Barsamian, "There is tons of work to be done, and lots of people who would like to do the work. It's just that the economic system is such a grotesque catastrophe that it can't even put together idle hands and needed work, which would be satisfying to the people and which would be beneficial to all of us. That's just the mark of a failed system. The most dramatic mark of it."

While many people have been very well trained to acknowledge that the system we have is the best system ever (and some even follow those boasts with high fives), the truth is that our system is incredibly fallible, right down to its roots. And we are going to have to give some serious thought about how we would like to move forward from here.

"Here's the essential point," writes Gar Alperovitz in *What Then Must We Do? Straight Talk About The Next American Revolution*, "a system problem - as opposed to your usual garden variety political problem - is one that isn't going to go away through politics as usual. It will require somehow changing the way things are rigged deeper down in the machinery of institutions, corporations, bureaucracy, and all the other elements of the system that produce the outcomes we experience. A system problem is difficult. It runs deep."

Considering the depth of our problem, the easiest thing to do is to ignore it and just uphold the status quo. After all, facing this problem is going to take some hard work, not only on the systemic level, but at the deep, interpersonal level as well. As many have done in the past, many would rather just shrug it off and do nothing but toe the line.

"All of us have a vested interest in pessimism," continues Alperovitz. "We don't have to do anything if nothing can be done!"

Again, we're human. Mistakes are in our methodology. However, it is not too late for course correction. If we're secure enough to accept that the system we've invested our time and talents into isn't perfect, then we should be able to open up to the idea that there could be a better way. As long as we open up to that possibility, then a better way is possible. But if we can't even imagine it, then it probably isn't there.

To find the answer we're looking for to our global problem, we're going to have to start looking closer to home. While the soft science of economics is indeed impressive, and offers many large numbers to impress the simple-minded, the true art of living starts where you are. To truly face the challenges before us, we have to face the challenges before us. That means starting in our own lives and our local communities instead of relying on the trickle-down assistance we've so often been promised but never fully received.

"We must learn to think in terms of an articulated structure that can cope with a multiplicity of small-scale units," says Ernst F. Schumacher. "If economic thinking cannot grasp this it is useless. If it cannot get beyond its vast abstractions, the national income, the rate of growth, capital/output ratio, input-output analysis, labour mobility, capital accumulation; if it cannot get beyond all this and make contact with the human realities of poverty, frustration, alienation, despair, breakdown, crime, escapism, stress, congestion, ugliness and spiritual death, then let us scrap economics and start afresh."

Since the word *homo sapiens* is translated to mean "wise person", it is high time we started practicing more wisdom while this planet still continues to entertain this species. Should we continue in our agreement, acquiescence, and apathy toward the systematic destruction of the human race by making the majority of us unable to live our best lives in the present or unable to live at all in the future, the planet will certainly not remember us as wise persons, but merely a pesky population of parasites that came and went like a rash as it makes its way through another rotation of the universe. We would be wise to realize that we don't need to live this way.

First Things First

if we ant to fix our global economy
there are a few things we need to consider
before we get too excited
and our hearts get all a-twitter
the first thing we need to realize
about this thing that we call money
is that it came from our imagination
just like the easter bunny
every mark put in a ledger
every euro, yen, and penny
every dollar, peso, rupee, and pound
the forms money takes are many
but the reality is that we made them all up
they sprouted from our minds
we would be wise to best learn how to use them
if we'd like to take the time
to consider the larger economy
beyond the market we invented
the economy that truly defines who we are
as a people and a planet
because we're more than just what we buy and sell
we are more than the things we make
and we are certainly more than money
it is high time that we wake
up to the reality before us

that we've been caught up in our obsession
with sacrificing reality and the world we live in
for the sake of our most ubiquitous invention
but if we can take a deep breath
and realize the breath doesn't cost us
it may help us to recognize
how we've been taken hostage
to the way we use money and the debt it creates
and how it mostly serves the wealthy
the way we push ourselves and the planet's limits
really isn't healthy
but our very breath can free us
and bring us to the now
where we can give thanks
to those who have gone before us
and realize they didn't know how
to build an economy any better than we do
and they certainly made mistakes
but we built traditions on their bad habits
and it's our responsibility to break
the patterns that are no longer serving us
and the ones that are wearing us down
because a global economy affects everyone
every person in every country in every town
while markets are very helpful
we got to realize that life is more
we got to think about who we really are
right down to our core
we are emotions and minds, bodies and spirits
we are simple and we are complex
and as we move forward
to build this world together
let's remember that life is a gift

WHAT WE HAVE GOING FOR US

"By relying primarily on voluntary co-operation and private enterprise, in both economic and other activities, we can insure that the private sector is a check on the powers of the governmental sector and an effective protection of freedom of speech, of religion, and of thought."
-Milton Friedman, *Capitalism and Freedom*

Even as we name all of the problems, it is more essential to propose solutions to them. This is exactly the purpose of ABC^2 Economics. But ABC^2 Economics is not *the* solution, only part of it.

A few years ago, I had the pleasure to meet Charles Eisenstein. I was about halfway through reading *Sacred Economics* at the time. He was passing through town and had agreed to stop and have lunch with a few people from Transition Sarasota.

I gave him a quick pitch on the idea behind ABC^2 Economics, but to my dismay, he didn't take to the idea as excitedly as I'd hoped. Instead, he told me that he believed that the days of movements led by one person, like Facebook or Microsoft, were over. From here on out, collaboration would be key.

To be honest, I don't really consider ABC^2 Economics to be my idea. I just looked at what society's been doing for the last ten thousand years and tried to find some semblance of agreement and balance. There is a good chance that I've never had an original thought in my head, I just rehash what I experience in interesting ways.

That said, I do agree that there are a variety of things that are going to work together to help us through the crises of our crumbling economic system. Fortunately, we have many auspicious realizations that can assist us in solving the problems we face.

For a person of true faith, or even someone with high hopes, it might even seem to be that for every problem we seem to have, life has also provided the tools we need to overcome it. How we utilize our advantages will be a deciding factor in whether this generation will develop a Renaissance or Dark Age. Let's look at some of the possibilities that face us, which could allow us to prosper rather than break down.

- Communication devices have created a global economy and a networked populace more connected than any previous time in known human history.
- The rise of networked society and social media offers endless opportunities for organization and communication, despite the plethora of abuses and misuses throughout it.
- Open source technologies have developed new means for collaborative ventures and the sharing economy.

- The proliferation of new crypto and complementary currencies offers many new avenues for people to achieve well-being that is not dependent upon the waning financial structures of hierarchies and indebtedness.
- Advancements in transactional technologies like blockchain now provide the opportunity for near-instantaneous transfers of money, information, and other currencies, including regularly scheduled microtransactions.
- More than 50% of the population is expected to be a freelancer by the year 2027, empowering a generation to focus their energies into purpose and good service rather than mere employment in meaningless jobs.
- Ranked-choice/instant-runoff voting has started to be used in statewide elections in Maine and New York City and could be used to drastically improve the political process throughout the country by ultimately overcoming the limitations of the two party system.
- Despite the adherence to fossil-fuel industries, development of renewable resources, alternative energy, and green technology continues to advance around the world.
- A growing consciousness has empowered a broader world view and a renewed spiritual

connection, beyond the doctrines and dogmas of religion.

- The breakdown of traditional values and religions have left many seeking greater purpose through a new, more participatory mythology.

We have a lot of things going for us now that did not exist in the 17th century, when capitalism had its start. As a matter of fact, many of the things we take for granted today couldn't have even been dreamed of by the founders of our country and framers of the US Constitution. We should bear that in mind as we move forward, releasing some of the limitations that have been programmed into the system we're serving.

If nothing else, we need to recognize the internet for the game changer that it really is. For although it has allowed capitalism to thrive by enabling the dotcom boom and bust, as well as building up some of the largest corporations ever known to man, the internet has also empowered the sharing economy and given people access to all sorts of goods, services, and information for free. If capitalism weren't held in such high esteem, perhaps it could do even more.

"Until we had shareable information goods," writes Paul Mason in *Postcapitalism: A Guide To Our Future*, "the basic law of economics was that everything is scarce. Supply and demand assumes scarcity. Now certain goods are not scarce, they are abundant - so supply and demand become irrelevant. The supply of an iTunes track is ultimately one file on a server in Cupertino, technically shareable by everyone. Only intellectual property law and a small piece of code in the iTunes track prevent everybody on Earth from owning every piece of music ever made. Apple's mission statement, properly expressed, is to prevent the abundance of music."

Yet beyond the manufactured scarcity still practiced by capitalist corporations, "The internet is a participatory gift economy," says Charles Eisenstein in *Sacred Economics*, "the P2P (peer to peer) network in which there is no consistent distinction between a producer and a consumer. When we share news, product recommendations, songs, and so forth with our online networks, we do not charge another for our 'information services.' It is a gift economy. The content of most websites is free as well."

Or as Kevin Kelly points out in *The Inevitable: Understanding the 12 Technological Forces That Will Shape Our Future*, "The internet is less a creation dictated by economics than one dictated by sharing gifts."

As we open ourselves to the Wisdom Revolution, we have the capacity to realize that life is more abundant than the limitations of the market and its invisible hand would like us to believe as long as we use wisdom in dealing with it. As such, we should embrace ways and means of celebrating this abundance beyond the limitations of the past, or those we keep dragging into the present. Not only should we realize the power of the Gift Economy, but in addition to dollars, our mainstream economy should include bitcoins, time dollars, and other digitized currencies.

We have the capacity to harness our digital developments of electricity and information to optimize labor and material, and develop a more interdependent economy. It really comes down to what our goals are and what the purpose of our economy is.

"The quest for a new economics begins with a simple question for which the answer should be obvious," says David Korten in *Change The Story, Change The Future: A Living Economy For A Living Earth*. "Is the purpose of the economy to maximize the profits of money-seeking corporate robots or the health and well-being of living households?"

We need a new economic model that allows currency to flow where we desire rather than being distorted by the self-centered gains of the elite. The ABC^2 Economics model is based on the flow of nature to ensure greater sustainability than the current system, which often works in opposition to nature. By working with our planet and realizing we are actually part of it, we can develop a sustainable, resilient quality of life for humanity and the rest of the world.

"If we were to establish a worldwide industrial system that harmonized with nature," says Daniel Pinchbeck in *How Soon is Now: From Personal Initiation to Global Transformation*, "enhancing the biodiversity and resilience, the superorganism of humanity would become a kind of a 'supernature'. We should make it our mission to create a hyper complex planetary civilization perfectly integrated with the Earth's ecology. If this seems impossible to achieve, perhaps that is because we are only now turning our focus in this direction. Many things that once seemed impossible have been accomplished by human willpower and imagination."

Although humanity has certainly made a mess of the planet with this economic system of endless growth, we have also created some truly incredible inventions and made some brilliant innovations. Fortunately, we still have the capacity to innovate and invent. Whatever acts of genius we come up with next to empower people to do purposeful work of service through their Artistry, Business, Citizenry, and Community, ABC^2 Economics serves to upgrade our activities by helping to channel the flow we create and create a more vibrant, yet manageable, economy.

"We can think of our current civilization," says Daniel Pinchbeck in *How Soon is Now: From Personal Initiation to Global Transformation*, "its technical and socio-political infrastructure, its ideology and beliefs - as an operating system, much like the software that runs our computers. Now we need to reboot and install a new system software. A new social design could, eventually, give every human being the opportunity to flourish and thrive, to live creatively, without fear for their future. Accomplishing this is a great mission that will require a truly rational, empathic application of our technical and creative powers."

ABC^2 Economics helps us recognize that the true economy, the truly global economy, consists of more than the blips of light and information that we call money. The true economy consists not only of the artistry, business, citizenry, and community we create, but also of the water, air, earth, and fire that creates us. As we represent these things through the use of money, may we use this tool with more wisdom than children in a sandbox.

IF I WERE ELECTED PRESIDENT

if you can believe it, i've had a number of people
who've said that i would make a good president
and to even consider entertaining
such a ridiculous idea
i have had my share of reticence
but after the nonsense i've seen in my lifetime
ranging from horrible to comical
i figure there's no way that i could do worse
and you just never know what's possible
and while i think it's highly unlikely
because our system is most certainly rigged
but if i could make my way
past the two parties in power
this is what i would bring
if i were elected president
the first thing i would do
after my inauguration
and all of the hullabaloo
i would start to build a cabinet
that was open to expansion
to include all of we the people
i think the government needs a new branch
and i know some will say
that makes the government bigger
and they don't want to see that increase

but because we're growing in people
we're growing in conflicts
and we could sure use the department of peace
beyond olives branches, doves,
the buddha, and hippies
but a confabulation of all of those things
a true beloved community
an organization of what makes our hearts sing
with technology that is open sourced
we would begin to build a platform
to help us communicate better
on how to make life an art form
and inside this department
the fourth to help balance the three
like our hearts, it would have four parts of its own
to create the flow that we need
the department of creativity celebrates the arts
the humanity of expression
and what makes us who we are
this department helps us to innovate
to educate and collaborate too
it is where we cultivate laughter and tears
to tell a new story about me and you
because we're more than just parts of a market
but that's important too
so the department of commerce
is assigned with the task
of helping the economy bloom
currently there are a number of ways
that we can trade and share
to value abundance over scarcity
this department helps make us aware
of which resources are here or there

and what everybody needs
and as we transition
from being such mindless consumers
we form the department of citizenry
wisely, we realize we require this planet
if we hope to continue the life of our species
we've got to think a lot more about resilience
and we've got to think about sustainability
because it's ridiculously stupid
to turn everything into garbage
simply to profit a few
to realize greater wealth in the people we are
is what the department of community will do
in community we realize we are all one
and we help take care of each other
because through both the water and spirit
that flows through us all
we are all sisters and brothers
so my platform would be a platform
in my presidential bid
to make our government based on our hearts,
minds, bodies, and spirits
just like our creator did

THE FOUR ECONOMIES

"Ecological harmony is a nonmarket value
that takes a collective will to achieve."
- Donald Worster - *Wealth of Nature:
Environmental History and the Ecological Imagination*

Economics 101 teaches that there are four basic types of economic systems: the Traditional Economic System, the Command Economic System, the (Free) Market Economic System, and the Mixed Economic System. While it's important to look at each one to see how humans have developed the civilization we're dealing with, beyond the systems we've created, there are three types of economies that don't usually get discussed in the classroom, but must be brought to light and considered.

When we think of primitive cultures, or second and third world countries, we see Traditional Economic Systems at work. They're fairly sustainable in that they're largely concerned with just developing enough for everyone to get by and have a relatively low environmental footprint as compared to other economic systems. People have roles they play and tasks they perform, but they are much less regimented than other economic systems, and people generally have more free time, but fewer entertainment luxuries to fill it with.

A Command Economic System is when the state runs things, as in communist Russia or China. When the government owns the means of production, the roles and tasks become jobs people must work in order to be provided for by the government. On the downside, there's not a lot of room for individuality or incentive for innovation, but on the plus side, it is more concerned with resource development and distribution.

The (Free) Market Economic System is what many Americans like to think America is. It's when the market runs the economy, unfettered by government interference, often referred to as *laissez-faire* economics. Fortunately, the U.S. government has made some rules to restrict the market, but it has also done a lot to enable and embolden market forces, which has led to a lot of pollution, exploitation, inequality, and waste.

Lastly, there's the Mixed Economic System, which integrates the Command and Market Economic Systems. This is what you see happening in the majority of developed countries, including America. The government and market run things, and they generally pay some lip service to traditional ways in nostalgic recollections.

The challenge with all of these economic systems is the same challenge we have with the study of economics as a whole. They exist within a silo and are unable to account for that which is beyond their purview. Unfortunately, that is most of the stuff that really matters.

The study of economics, like psychology, sociology, and linguistics, is often referred to as a "soft" science. Natural sciences, like biology, chemistry, and geology, are considered "hard" due to their characteristics of quantifiable data, objective accuracy, replicable experimentation, and their ability to fully utilize the scientific method. But "soft" sciences basically deal with the social patterns of *homo sapiens*, which are often erratic, temperamental, unpredictable, and random.

Largely, the science of economics uses mathematics to develop patterns for the uses of goods and services through humanity's most sacred creation, money. While many have been led to believe that money is the most important substance in the world (even though it has no real substance), and its endless growth is the surest sign of success and human achievement (regardless of the impact upon the rest of the world), the unfortunate reality is that the soft science of economics doesn't have the scientific capacity to process the data of the hard world beyond its tunnel vision. Basically, the economic systems heretofore considered by mainstream economics only account for a very small portion of the actual economy.

The actual economy consists of four different economies:

- The Market Economy
- The Core Economy
- The Planetary Economy
- The Gift Economy

The Market Economy

There is good reason that the Market Economy receives so much attention from humans and is largely considered to be what economics is all about. It's a pretty incredible phenomenon, and has been incredibly instrumental in developing what we consider human civilization. It includes everything we buy and sell as we create the art of our lives.

Both the (Free) Market and Command Economic Systems are part of The Market Economy. From the perspective of capitalism, and its dream of the (Free) Market Economic System, this consists of the four roles of business owner-operator, consumer, worker, and government. The Command Economic System seems to merge the roles of business owner-operator with government and consumer with worker. Both methods are still largely focused on only a portion of human life, the marketplace, and fail to take in the greater picture.

As the hard sciences of biology, chemistry, and geology can attest, there are many other things occurring in the world outside the marketplace. Because the science of economics is incapable of recognizing them, much less addressing them, even though it is a soft science, its misuse creates effects that are very hard for the rest of the world to adapt to. And treating it like a hard science, as most militant capitalists and communists do, forces the Core Economy, Planetary Economy, and Gift Economy to endure whatever short-sighted, ill-conceived methodology *homo sapiens* conjure up in our attempts to control the world by turning it all into one big "free" marketplace that transmogrifies everything into our most beloved creation, money.

"The marketplace is an institution that teaches self-advancement, private acquisition, and the domination of nature," says Donald Worster in *Wealth of Nature: Environmental History and the Ecological Imagination*. "Its way of thinking is incompatible with the round river."

Our society's veneration of the market has manipulated our individual and collective goals so much that the accumulation of wealth as measured by money has largely become our highest priority. We have, in many ways, shirked our responsibility as caretakers of the Earth. Instead, we have sought to strip her of everything, much of which we barely understand, in order to turn it all into the more managable, quantifiable, understandable, and near ubiquitous human creation, money. Unfortunately, while many see the folly in our ways, we feel powerless to do anything about it, and even beholden to continuing our contributions to the system that seems determined to usher in our own destruction.

In *Agenda For A New Economy*, David Korten describes our current Market Economic System as, "a morally bankrupt money system accountable only to itself, detached from reality, and driven by unadulterated individualistic greed and a misconception of wealth and money that favors those who create phantom wealth for those who need and deserve it least at the expense of those with real needs doing beneficial work."

For the humans who want their grandchildren to have any sort of quality of life, it is imperative to recognize that the Market Economy is of human creation and not the most important facet of life. Considering that *homo sapiens* have only existed for a very small percentage of life on this planet, what we know of as money has only existed for about 10% of our species' existence, and the economic system we now serve has only been in place for a few hundred years, roughly 3% of our use of money. In the grand scheme of things, another way of doing things is not out of the question, but mostly how things have always been done. All progress is based on doing things in ways they haven't been done before.

"It's time we stop confusing the practice of moving money around with generating real wealth," says Richard Florida in *The Great Reset*. "If we want to prosper again, we'll need to move the economy away from finance capitalism and back toward the aptly dubbed real economy - investing once again in technology and human capital along with the new infrastructure that can make long-term economic growth possible."

In order to see beyond the myopia of the market, we have to look at what else life has to offer beyond the game of money and the Market Economy. Fortunately, the Core Economy has been providing for human needs for the entirety of our species' existence and the Planetary Economy has been building for millions of years, making all of this possible in the first place. Perhaps we should seek to understand them more and invest more of ourselves into economies with much greater endurance before we sacrifice them both to the false gods of the marketplace.

The Core Economy

The Market Economy is easy to understand due to its reliance on money, which allows for simple quantifications and record-keeping. It's about measurements, which appeals to the simple yet competitive part of ourselves. The Core Economy is not as easily measured, and although it may actually be much more simple than the Market Economy, it is not as easy to understand.

The Core Economy is what Professor Edgar Kahn calls that 40-50% of productive economic activity that takes place outside of the market and is not measured by traditional indicators. "It probably doesn't do anything important from the point of GDP," Kahn says. "It just raises children, makes neighborhoods safe and vibrant, raises strong families, takes care of the elderly, gets involved in things like elections, tries to make democracy work, tries to make officials accountable, fights for social justice, tries to keep the planet sustainable, but nothing of economic importance you understand."

Ultimately, the Core Economy is what drove human civilization for almost 200,000 years until we invented money and developed the Market Economy in order to keep track of things. The Core Economy isn't as insistent on keeping track of things. It's largely grounded in the idea of family so there's not a real strong push to account for who owns what when everything is shared, or for who owes what since everything is forgiven.

In large part, the Core Economy is what empowered the Traditional Economic System, and continues to empower it today in a number of communities and less developed countries around the world. And even in technologically advanced countries that more fully embrace the ideologies of the Market Economy, the Core Economy still serves as the foundation upon which the Market Economy exists. It is important to remember that without the Core Economy, the Market Economy would have no foundation upon which it could build.

"By largely ignoring the core economy, mainstream economics has also overlooked just how much the paid economy depends upon it," says Kate Raworth in *Doughnut Economics*. "Without all that cooking, washing, nursing and sweeping, there would be no workers - today or in the future - who were healthy, well fed and ready for work each morning."

Because caring for one another cannot be quantified, because there are parts of existence we do not wish to offer up as commodities and sell, because we intrinsically want to operate out of love and give more than we receive, the Core Economy is simultaneously too complex and simple for the methodology of the Market Economy to process. And of course, it is completely incapable of factoring in the Planetary Economy, without which, neither the Core Economy nor the Market Economy would exist.

The Planetary Economy

The Market Economy is designed so that whomever owns or claims rights to a portion of the planet gets to lay claim to whatever resources that property may have and sell them as products. In all of the writings produced by humanity, at least what we have at our disposal, ever since men started keeping track of things, instituting the Market Economy, it has never been made clear from whom the first owners of any given piece of property purchased it from to begin with or how they claimed the rights to it. And while the Market Economy has been pivotal for many of humanity's innovations and triumphs over the last few thousand years, the foundation of ignorance it is built upon has resulted in much damage to the Planetary Economy.

As environmental advocate Lester Brown said, "Socialism failed because it couldn't tell the economic truth; capitalism failed because it couldn't tell the ecological truth."

While some would say that capitalism has not failed, but remains as the best economic system ever, they are largely screaming this from inside the bubble of the Market Economy and remain largely unaware that the Planetary Economy exists. But because capitalism is incapable of quantifying the effects it has on the planet as it continues to use property rights to turn resources into waste to produce money, although it can't account for it, it causes irreparable damages.

"Whenever we engage in consumption or production patterns which take more than we need," Vandana Shiva explains in *Earth Democracy: Justice, Sustainability, and Peace*, "we are engaging in violence."

"As the world's resources of non-renewable fuels—coal, oil, and natural gas—are exceedingly unevenly distributed over the globe and undoubtedly limited in quantity," E.F. Schumacher agrees, "it is clear that their exploitation at an ever-increasing rate is an act of violence against nature which must almost inevitably lead to violence between men."

Of course, violence is nothing new to our species. And although there is nothing written about the very first real estate purchases, looking at the occurrences of history, much of the acquisition of property since was taken by violent force and then ushered into the Market Economy to produce debt and profits for generations to come. In addition, throughout the development of our Market Economy, people themselves have often been violently forced to participate in it or have been acquired to be property in it.

Yet violence against another person, or even a group of people, is one thing, but violence against our own planet is another. While person on person violence will still take its toll on our souls, the abuse we mete out on the planet is abuse against our very selves, as well as future generations. And although this violence may very well be unintentional and unnoticed by most of us, we should recognize the impact of our unconscious activities.

After all, as E.F. Schumacher pointed out, "The real problems of our planet are not economic or technical, they are philosophical. The philosophy of unbridled materialism is being challenged by events."

While adherents to the Market Economy don't often have a world view capable of recognizing issues like climate change and peak oil, those with eyes to see recognize that our system of consumerism is taking its toll on the planet and something needs to be done. What we need is a way for people to become part of the solution instead of merely bystanders for the end of life as we know it.

"This is the moment," says C. Otto Scharmer in *Leading from the Emerging Future: From Ego-System to Eco-System Economies*, "when what we need most is enough people with the skill, heart, and wisdom to help us pull ourselves back from the edge of breakdown and onto a different path."

The path of the Market Economy is not wide enough for all of us, and it will eventually reach a dead end. Since it was designed to convert all things into commodities, it has already turned a number of our Core Economy tasks into compensated jobs, like child care and care for the elderly, and it has proven that it will stop at nothing to transform every ounce of our natural resources into digits in a computer server.

"No compromise is possible between the values and power structures of the money economy and living economy systems," says David Korten in *Change The Story, Change The Future: A Living Economy For A Living Earth*. "Their differences are irreconcilable. There is no way to produce outsized financial returns to the assets of billionaires, allow the few to monopolize the control of and disrupt Earth's living systems for a quick profit, and simultaneously maintain the conditions essential to Earth's life and meet the needs of all."

Indeed, Market Economy adherents, especially those who've become the greatest addicts to the game of finance, will need to check themselves. Many people have been programmed to defend the notion of individual property rights as the single most important matter in human existence, and the unrestricted liberty to amass as much material wealth as possible, largely represented by numbers in a digital account, stands as a testament to our personal sovereignty. In other words, we have an ego problem on our hands.

For Market Economy fundamentalists, it would be beneficial to look back upon the early proponents of the system, and recognize what they saw as its truest purpose beyond ego aggrandizement.

As Daniel Bell point out in *The Cultural Contradictions of Capitalism*, "no moral philosopher, from Aristotle to Aquinas, to John Locke and Adam Smith, divorced economics from a set of moral ends or held the production of wealth to be an end in itself; rather it was seen as a means to the realization of virtue, a means of leading a civilized life."

To be fair, many in the Market Economy have virtue. Quite a few have a lot of it. Although the system doesn't lend itself to benevolence, many people in it do.

"For companies that want to pursue what has often been called the triple bottom line (emphasizing people and planet in addition to profit)," writes Gar Alperovitz in *What Then Must We Do? Straight Talk About The Next American Revolution*, "the traditional legal structure thus poses challenges - a reality that led private-equity expert Andrew Kassoy to join with two others to found B Lab and invent the B Corporation, a corporate structure that facilitates the use of business profits for social purposes. In a B Corp (also known as a benefit corporation) people who invest know from the outset that the goal is both to make profits and to use some part of them for social purposes."

Since B Corporations have become legitimized, as of this writing, laws permitting companies to charter themselves as B Corporations have been enacted in 34 states and Washington DC while 6 more have bills in motion, so far. While this is a great step in the right direction, it is one step in a long journey. Truly opening the Market Economy up to giving back to the Core and Planetary

Economy will also require a shift in our lifestyles and the ways in which we operate in the world.

The Gift Economy

Archeological records show that before humankind developed the Market Economy, our species lived a more egalitarian lifestyle where everything was shared. Living as nomads, early human tribes lived as one people rather than a group of individuals. Even in more modern primitive cultures, hoarding resources (so common in our society) is seen as a mental illness, and those afflicted with the inability to share are banished from the village.

Egalitarianism had a number of benefits in tribal society. Sharing with others ensured reciprocity when another tribe member found food or other resources. It relieved them of the burden of caring for and transporting surplus. And it provided them with the joy that comes from investing in others. Rather than accumulating material goods, they accumulated trust, appreciation, support, and love.

"Nonaccumulation models hunter-gatherer societies," says Charles Eisenstein in *Sacred Economics*, "in which there was great abundance but no accumulation, and in which prestige went to those who gave the most. To give the most, one also had to receive the most, either from nature or from other people. The great hunter, the skilled artist or musician, the energetic, the healthy, and the lucky would have more to give. In any event, this kind of prestige is to the benefit of all. It is only when high income translates into accumulation, frivolous consumption, or socially destructive consumption that it makes sense to restrict it. In other words, the problem is not with high income; it is with the results of the income getting stuck at some point in its circulation, accumulating and stagnating."

After all that humanity has been through, the Wisdom Revolution offers us the opportunity to embrace the entirety of our history, recognizing that both the individual and the whole of the planet is worthy to be cared for, and we're graced with the ability, through our own industriousness and the Provider of the lives we get to be industrious with, to share in the abundance beyond the limitations of the Market Economy.

"The sharing economy is also growing," says Kate Raworth in *Doughnut Economics*, "in which the culture of ownership - with every household equipped with its own washing machine and car is giving way to a culture of access, with households sharing laundry facilities and renting cars by the hour from a local car club. Rather than go shopping for new clothes, books and children's toys, a growing number of people are swapping - or 'swishing' - them with friends and neighbors. In such an economy, plenty of economic value will still be generated through the products and services that people enjoy, but far less of that total value will flow through market transactions."

The rise of the sharing economy has certainly made an impact in the Market Economy. It has completely disrupted the "old school" methods of capitalism, providing a number of paradoxical situations. For instance, Uber, the largest provider of transportation, owns no vehicles; AirBnB, the largest provider of temporary shelter, owns no residential property; YouTube, the largest distributor of video content, produces no content; Facebook, the largest provider of news, does no journalism; et cetera. Yet, it is also being seen as people use the technology at our disposal to not only share in the Market Economy, but also to simply share.

A number of websites have emerged, allowing people to share a variety of goods and services, not for monetary compensation, but just to spread the wealth that the wealthy haven't absorbed yet. For instance, couchsurfing.com connects people who need a couch to sleep on with people who want to have guests sleep on their couch; freecycle.com helps people with stuff to get rid of get in touch with people that want it... not for currency, just to keep materials in use and out of the landfill; and nearly every city in the civilized world has a few Facebook groups devoted to sharing goods and services... for free.

Complementary currencies like time-banking have also taken hold in a variety of communities, where people use their time as currency, allowing them to better invest in and realize the value of the Core Economy. With an online time bank, time-bankers can post services they offer and services they need, connecting with others in the community who need or want to offer help. However, many time-bankers, although they have the technology to track the number of hours given to another, don't bother logging them. Instead, they merely embrace the Gift Economy and allow the purpose they feel through service be its own reward.

The sharing economy, using technology to empower people to offer their goods and services in the Market Economy, is one thing, but the Gift Economy is its own entity. Even beyond the support offered through the Core Economy, the Gift Economy extends not only to those near and dear to us, those with whom we regularly create community, but to the rest of the world as well. The Gift Economy empowers people to fully realize freedom with the ability to give freely, releasing the fear and need for control that the Market Economy requires.

"The technological direction of this revolution is at odds with its social direction," writes Paul Mason in *Postcapitalism: A Guide To Our Future.* "Technologically, we are headed for zero price goods, unmeasurable work, an exponential takeoff in productivity and the extensive automation of physical processes. Socially, we are trapped in a world of monopolies, inefficiency, the ruins of a finance-dominated free market and a proliferation of 'bullshit jobs'. Today, the main contradiction in modern capitalism is between the possibility of free, abundant socially produced goods, and a system of monopolies, banks and governments struggling to maintain control over power and information. That is, everything is pervaded by a fight between network and hierarchy."

Human civilization has largely operated through hierarchies in the roughly 10,000 years since we invented money and the Market Economy. Although the population has served at the behest of kings, queens, emperors, sultans, dictators, presidents, councils, republics, and the ministers who have been given the power of punishment, there has also been a constant yearning to have more freedom from the rule of others and to develop a stronger sense of equality and interdependence through a more democratic network of relationships. And although the founders of the American experiment dreamed of creating a democracy, only with the technological developments of the last few decades have we had a glimmer of how an actual democracy could work.

As we redevelop what we know as the "economy", we would be wise to recognize the economic needs we have beyond the Market Economy. After a century of advertisements and marketing propaganda, our minds have been filled with manufactured desires and cravings, but what do we really need to live happy, fulfilling lives? While the tunnel vision of capitalism has had so many of us driven toward the individual acquisition of material goods and selfishness at all costs, those who can see beyond the trappings of personal vanity realize that human needs are more complex than mere ego cultivation.

"People don't need enormous cars," writes Donella H. Meadows in *The Limits to Growth: The 30-Year Update,* "they need admiration and respect. They don't need a constant stream of new clothes; they need to feel that others consider them to be attractive, and they need excitement and variety and beauty. People don't need electronic entertainment; they need something interesting to occupy their minds and emotions. And so forth. Trying to fill real but nonmaterial needs-for identity, community, self-esteem, challenge, love, joy-with material things is to set up an unquenchable appetite for false solutions to never-satisfied longings. A society that allows itself to admit and articulate its nonmaterial human needs, and to find nonmaterial ways to satisfy them, would require much lower material and energy throughputs and would provide much higher levels of human fulfillment."

In order to create the world we want, we are going to have to think bigger than the world view we've accepted over the last several millennia. While our Artistry and Business can easily be accounted for in the Market Economy as buyer and seller, to develop a more balanced economy, we must also realize and appreciate the value the Core Economy contributes toward our Citizenry and Community by investing in the Planetary Economy and making the Gift Economy possible.

"The generosity of the Earth allows us to feed all mankind," E.F. Schumacher reminds us in *A Guide for the Perplexed*, "we know enough about ecology to keep the Earth a healthy place; there is enough room on the Earth, and there are enough materials, so that everybody can have adequate shelter; we are quite competent enough to produce sufficient supplies of necessities so that no one need live in misery."

This is the goal of ABC^2 Economics.

THE POWER OF FOUR

now that we have the knowledge we do
we can look back at our history
by recognizing our patterns
we are granted with the liberty
to learn from the mistakes we've made
and try to correct our folly
and give more consideration
to what we're trying to embody
as we lead these lives we lead
we've got to know our limits
you can lead a man to a good idea
but you can't make him think it
but we can see what we've been thinking
and track our understanding
so the journey from what is to what if
need not be so demanding
because things always get complex
let's start out with the simple
and look at things upon which we agree
and the notions that are nimble
that have played out in patterns
throughout our history
and been woven through our traditions
so we can all come together
and make the most of this existence

to start out with the basics
nature has four elements
water, air, earth, and fire
are the foundation of our development
eventually, nature peopled
and humanity was made
crafted with heart, mind, body, and spirit
it seems we have displayed
an affinity for or understanding of
things that come in quartets
and if we follow the flow of the fabulous four
we may start to connect
in ways that have always been there
but we've managed to ignore
yet a whole lot of life has found its balance
by coming up with four
on a personal note, i have personal interest
so i just want to be upfront and honest
my fascination may have
something to do with the fact
that my birthday's on the fourth day of august
you should also know that when i was a kid
i was a 4-h club member
i learned about animals and agriculture
through the ridin' rednecks chapter
i pledged my hands to greater service
and my health to better living
my heart to greater loyalty
and my head to clearer thinking
i haven't always lived up to that
and there are many who could tell some stories
but i like to think i'm getting a better grasp of it
now that i'm in my forties

in math, four is the smallest number
that can be considered a composite
it's the base number of a plane
and that's probably because it's
the same number of directions
we can decide to go
and you always play music in four four time
when you want to rock and roll
we also have four limbs
and four chambers to our hearts
if you think that's incredible
just wait till i get started
we also have four blood types
and it goes even deeper
franklin delano roosevelt said
we also have four freedoms
there are four bases in baseball
other games have four periods
and there are quite a number of people
who take four letter words quite serious
if you look to the jewish tradition
god's name had four letters
the bible also has four gospels and horsemen
the garden of eden had four rivers
the buddha shared four noble truths
hindus have four scriptures
pyramids have four sides
and the i ching has four symbols
the arcana of the tarot
has four suits that seekers enjoy
following the mystical guidance
of cups, swords, wands, and coins
others may seek their fortunes in poker

through hearts, spades, clubs, and diamonds
and, of course, we have four seasons
to enjoy this changing climate
as we change with our changing world
if we want to be effective
we'll look at the patterns of history
and focus our directive
on the four roles stephen covey mentioned
as he spoke of the seven effective habits
he said, if you want to be a good leader
if you want to change your status
it starts when you direct the flow
and start to do what matters
as you become a director
you also start coaching others
if you give them the support they need
as they direct themselves
your ability to delegate
will be the only help
that is required from the people
that you have now empowered
by playing these four roles of leadership
and recognizing our
greatest goals as we live these lives
and carve out what will be our destiny
basically, we all want to love, learn, and live
and we also want to leave a legacy
i propose that we do just that
as we continue our evolution
let us embrace this way of balance
and invoke the wisdom revolution
we can direct our flow as artists of life
coaching others in our business

supporting each other as citizens
and delegating forgiveness
by realizing we're all just making our way
and doing the best we can
and while none of us is perfect
we're better than when we began
and we can use this power of four
to make life more dynamic
through our artistry, business,
citizenry, and community
we have abc squared economics

CULTIVATING LEADERSHIP THROUGH ABC² ECONOMICS

"Any intelligent fool can make things bigger,
more complex, and more violent.
It takes a touch of genius —
and a lot of courage to move in the opposite direction."
- E.F. Schumacher

The Market Economy has a conundrum. It is built upon the use of money, which exists to serve as a proxy for trust since people cannot be trusted. Unfortunately, the Market Economy is operated largely by people and corporations that have proven themselves untrustworthy, and who continue to point out the untrustworthiness of others.

It's a very challenging thing indeed to cultivate leadership in a system that is based on the notion of mistrust. While humanity has managed to pull it off in a variety of regards, it has not been without its fair share of environmental devastation, extreme poverty, violence, and war. However, considering that our civilization has largely been fixated on only about a quarter of what's possible (if that), should we have enough faith in our species to give it a little more credit, and invest in our other assets, we may find more value than the market alone allows.

"The essential fact about humans is that they are multidimensional beings," says Muhammad Yunus in *Building Social Business: The New Kind of Capitalism That Serves Humanity's Most Pressing Needs*. "Their happiness comes from many sources, not just from making money. And yet economists have built their whole theory of business on the assumption that human beings do nothing in their economic lives besides pursue selfish interests. The theory concludes that the optimal result for society will occur when each individual's search for selfish benefit is given free rein. This interpretation of human beings denies any role to other aspects of life—political, social, emotional, spiritual, environmental, and so on."

"At the heart of twentieth-century economics stands the portrait of rational economic man," explains Kate Raworth in *Doughnut Economics*, "he has told us that we are self-interested, isolated, calculating, fixed in taste and dominant over nature - and his portrait has shaped who we have become. But human nature is far richer than this, as early sketches of our new self-portrait reveal: we are social, interdependent, approximating, fluid in values and dependent upon the living world."

What if we developed an economic system that could cultivate trust? What if we promoted greater transparency so that we would have nothing to hide? What if we realized that people, considering that they comprise the entirety of the human population, are more trustworthy than the Market Economy and its manipulative methods of disinformation have allowed us to believe?

"If the world were full of the self-seeking individuals found in economics textbooks," clarifies award-winning economist Ha-Joon Chang in *23 Things They Don't Tell You About Capitalism*, "it would grind to a halt because we would be spending most of our time cheating, trying to catch the cheaters, and punishing the caught. The world works as it does only because people are not the totally self seeking agents that free-market economics believes them to be. We need to design an economic system that, while acknowledging that people are often selfish, exploits other human motives to the fullest and gets the best out of people. The likelihood is that, if we assume the worst about people, we will get the worst out of them."

For a number of reasons, there is a mainstream distrust for humanity running throughout humanity. Although we've been encouraged to be very proud of our achievements, our countries, and the bustling civilization we contribute to, as a whole, we still don't seem to think much of humans. The general, underlying sentiment is that humans are inherently lazy, selfish, and competitive, and they must be made to work or there will be trouble.

However, as Kate Raworth says in *Doughnut Economics*, "*Homo sapiens*, it turns out, is the most cooperative species on the planet, outperforming ants, hyenas, and even the naked mole-rat when it comes to living alongside those who are beyond our next of kin."

What if we chose to start focusing on more of the good in humanity? What if we developed an economy that rewarded doing the right thing instead of disregarding it as is so often the case in in the Market Economy? What if we started recognizing people as more than just consumers?

"The human capacity to choose is perhaps the most distinctive characteristic of our nature," says David Korten in *Agenda For A New Economy*. "What we are depends in substantial measure on what we choose to be - not just by our individual choices but also by how we shape the collective cultures and institutions that in turn shape our individual behavior."

That is, after all, one of the benefits of living through this age of technological advancement and the capabilities it allows. Although we do get to explore the development of artificial intelligence, we also have the capacity to study human intelligence, not only cognitive intelligence, but our emotional, social, and environmental intelligence as well.

Kevin Kelly said in *The Inevitable*, "The funny thing about a whole class of technology that enhances experience and personalization is that it puts great pressure on us to know who we are."

As we redevelop our economy, let's give some thought to what we really want for humanity. Certainly, we're smart enough to realize the limitations of only supporting the Market Economy. Let's open up to the abundance that is truly our birthright, and recognize the wealth of the Core Economy, the Planetary Economy, and the Gift Economy.

"We wasted two hundred years staring at the wrong portrait of ourselves: *Homo economicus*," says Kate Raworth in *Doughnut Economics*, "that solitary figure poised with money in his hand, calculator in his head, nature at his feet, and an insatiable appetite in his heart. It is time to redraw ourselves as people who thrive by connecting with each other and with this living home of ours that is not ours alone."

It may very well be that we have been offered the technological advances that we have because we are ready to use them. Perhaps human evolution is at the place where it is ready to make a change and redirect its energy from the rampant consumerism that the Market Economy requires to the participatory citizenship the rest of the world needs. The proof, as they say, will be in the pudding.

"Revolution doesn't happen when society adopts new technologies," Clay Shirky reminds us in *Here Comes Everybody: The Power of Organizing Without Organizations*, "it happens when society adopts new behaviors."

Moving forward, may we recognize that *homo sapiens*' highest purpose is not to make money. We are gifted with so many other capacities and talents that can enrich the Core Economy, tend to the Planetary Economy, and contribute to the Gift Economy. Let us consider how we can empower citizens to participate in each of these facets of our world, rather than continuing to merely enslave them in the marketplace.

"We need to reconceive the idea of a good society in the early twenty-first century and to find a creative path toward it," says Jeffrey D. Sachs in *The Price Of Civilization: Reawakening American Virtue And Prosperity*. "Most important, we need to be ready to pay the price of civilization through multiple acts of good citizenship: bearing our fair share of taxes, educating ourselves deeply about society's needs, acting as vigilant stewards for future generations, and remembering that compassion is the glue that holds society together."

And for those who have been trained to long for the fast life that capitalism has promised through its commercials and advertisements, promising all of the personal freedom and happiness you can possibly consume, provided you can afford it, a new path forward won't be as boring as you may think. As a matter of fact, it will be much healthier for both the individual and the collective.

"We don't think a sustainable society need be stagnant, boring, uniform, or rigid," Donella H. Meadows, Jorgen Randers, and Dennis Meadows assure us in their 30 year update to *The Limits to Growth*. "It need not be, and probably could not be, centrally controlled or authoritarian. It could be a world that has the time, the resources, and the will to correct its mistakes, to innovate, to preserve the fertility of its planetary ecosystems. It could focus on mindfully increasing quality of life rather than on mindlessly expanding material consumption and the physical capital stock."

In his book *People, Power, and Profits: Progressive Capitalism for an Age of Discontent*, Nobel Prize Winning economist Joseph Stiglitz proclaims, "We as a country can prosper only if there is shared prosperity: this is both an economic reality and an expression of deeply held values. This new social contract should include a commitment that every individual has the opportunity to live up fully to his or her potential, and that every person's voice is heard in our democracy."

As we develop a more effective means of creating our economy and empowering one another, and as we reconsider the goals for humanity, we should also consider the goals of each human. Stephen Covey, author of *The 7 Habits of Highly Effective People*, says that there are four roles of leadership. What if we lead humanity toward cultivating a system that would encourage people to play those roles to the fullest?

Covey says the first role is that of *Directing*, where we direct our energy, our attention, and our time to create the lives that we lead and impact others around us. We move on to the role of *Coaching*, sharing and teaching lessons we have learned, alchemizing our passions to truly serve the needs of others. We take on the role of *Supporting* others, taking care of our people, our planet, and all the life it provides. And finally, through the role of *Delegating*, we encourage others to carry on our missions and expand our legacy of service.

In order to embrace the greater economy and empower people to find their place in it, we'll need to be able to sort through our new social arrangements and organize. In his 2008 book *Here Comes Everybody*, media theorist Clay Shirky suggests a useful hierarchy, ranked by the increasing degree of coordination employed. Groups of people start off simply sharing with a minimum of coordination, and then progress to cooperation, then to collaboration, and finally to collectivism. At each step of this socialism, the amount of additional coordination required enlarges.

Setting up his *Agenda For A New Economy*, David Korten says, "We can reallocate resources from the military to healthcare and environmental rejuvenation, from automobiles to public transportation, from mining to recycling, from suburban sprawl to compact communities and the reclamation of the forest and agricultural lands, from advertising to education, and from financial speculation to local entrepreneurship - to name just a few immediate priorities. This reallocation is the key to reducing the aggregate human burden on Earth while simultaneously improving health and happiness."

We have the capacity to not only build and restore trust among one another, but to also encourage the best behaviors and highest ideals. The future is ours to shape. What sort of leadership do we wish to provide?

the wisdom revolution

a transaction was once thought to be
an exchange between buyer and seller
but that's like saying that banking
is just about the teller
now we know there's a whole lot more
that goes in to each transaction
every purchase we make
sets off a chain reaction
of how we create more supply
to comply with every demand
and who does what with what we've got
but we've got to understand
that not all demands are worthy
and we need not cater to them
some resonate with lower vibrations
and scientists have proven
that life exists outside the bounds
of our mythical free market
and a higher quality of life
should really be our target
as we stand here in the now
and aim into the future
can we envision our species as more
than merely mindless consumers

while it's true
that when you appeal to our base desires
and spur it along with manipulation
we'll follow along and buy what you're selling
and we'll often give in to temptation
when you inflate and deflate our egos
and mix in some manufactured scarcity
and promote greed and fear and competition
it's the perfect recipe
for taking advantage
of the selfishness we're born with
and the instinct for self-interest
but if there's more to life then there's more to us
and there are ways that can be different
what if we built an economy
on the abundance that we have
if we realize life is more than a market
there's no limit to the things we can
achieve when we realize who we are
at our very core
we are friends and family and community members
and the people that live next door
we are the relationships we cultivate
and the environments we maintain
and if the power went out
and all the money was gone
we are what would remain
and here we are on this life-giving planet
and for this moment we exist
i've said it before and i'll say it again
life is such a gift

imagine if we had the power
to direct the flow of our transactions
what if we could guide our money
to make what we want happen
what if, when we were paid
our money was channeled automatically
because when it all comes down to it
it's only information and energy
what if we can use it more wisely
than the models to which we're beholden
where the elite have all of the money and power
so they also have all the control and
the rest of us don't have much say
on how we move forward together
but based on the human innovation i've seen
i think we the people can do better
considering how we've balanced things out before
there are four variables to our economy
how we practice the art of living
through our business, citizenry, and community
so let's begin with the end in mind
and realize we're all one big global community
the spirit of life infuses us all
and now may be all we'll ever know of eternity
but we know we're all connected
we know we're all sisters and brothers
and if we're going to realize
a life of resilient abundance
there's no need for so many to suffer
so let us all agree right now
the things we do have consequence
what if every economic interaction we make
serves to lift up human consciousness

as churches have done for ages
with their tithes and other offerings
what if 10% of every transaction
went to heal the world and alleviate suffering
we don't have to be religious
to want to give back and help out the needy
and when you're living a truly abundant life
there's just no need to be so greedy
since each of us are different
and we each have different passions
we each get to choose what we support
which endeavors, organizations, and actions
what if we could change how much we give
because some of us may want to give more
some of us have realized the joy that comes
by serving the homeless, the sick, and the poor
the truth is we're already doing this
but we can do it much more fluidly
because if we want
the money in our economy to flow
we've got to treat it like a currency
if we automate the golden rule
by channeling some of our energy
to our community
what if we also participate in the world
by channeling some of it to our citizenry
as it stands, governments take our money
to pay the house and senate
they do a lot of things we don't want them to do
as they decide how they can best spend it
with bigger countries, there's a lot of waste
as they let the money trickle down

to the people who really need it
but what if we could turn that around
what if we could decide where our support goes
what if we start from the bottom up
what if we invest first in our local communities
would the system be less corrupt
if we could choose
the initiatives we want to support
and have public servants who follow the will
of, by, and for the people
was how things were promised
but we're still trying to fulfill
the potential of those people
and the power of participation
it could very well be that democracy
is going to require a bit more engagement
most of us have the wherewithal to know
that governments should work for humans
but we've still got quite a few tweaks to make
before this is a more perfect union
for quite a long while
we've been led to believe
that to be a good citizen
is to support the government
but there's a greater loyalty we should consider
with our planet we should make a new covenant
while we should patronize our various governments
for as long as they are relevant
as good citizens
we should take better care of the earth
and try to use some more intelligence
on how we use the resources we have
of time and space and nature

and for all that we've screwed up so far
we should start buying it back by the acre
what if we expand our forests
plant more seeds and let life grow
invest in wilderness and diversity
just imagine what we could sow
while it's true we're a global community
life's about much more than humans
embracing that knowledge is a very big part
of the wisdom revolution

THE FOUR ASPECTS OF BEING AND NATURE

"Every human has four endowments -
self awareness, conscience, independent will, and creative imagination.
These give us the ultimate human freedom...
The power to choose, to respond, to change."
- Stephen Covey

The four roles of leadership that Dr. Covey presented were linked to the four basic aspects of humanity, and what he referred to as the four goals of life. *To love* is the primary goal of our *hearts*, and as leaders, we *direct* the flow of our lives to what we love. *To learn* is the activity of our *mind*, and as leaders, we *coach* others based on what we know. *To live* is why we have a *body*, and as leaders, we *support* our community with good health and enjoyable activities. And *to leave a legacy*, our *spirit* goes on beyond us, and our leadership is *delegate*d to future generations.

Yet these parts of ourselves are also reflective of the natural elements that comprise us.

For instance, while the heart represents our *emotional* body, it is also the muscle that ensures our physical body has a constant flow of blood, comprised largely of *water*. When water evaporates, it forms clouds in the *air*, and according to comic strips, that's where our *mind* gets its best ideas. Obviously, our *body* is made of *earth* and will return to it. And our *spirit* is the *fire* that gives us the energy to live.

While this is largely metaphorical, it is a metaphor that has run throughout a number of traditions and helped to build our cultural understanding in a variety of ways.

As an example, let's look at a common deck of playing cards. The four suits are said to represent the four pillars of the economy of the Middle Ages. The *hearts* represented the Church. The *spades* represented the Military. The *clubs* represented Agriculture. And the *diamonds* represented the Merchants.

While our current economic system differs greatly from that of the Middle Ages, the cards are still representative of the four human aspects. *Hearts* are pretty obvious. The *spade* digs for the truth the *mind* seeks. The *club* still works the *earth*. And *diamonds* radiate the splendor and mystery of *spirit*.

In the suits of the Tarot deck, there is similar symbology. The *cups* bear water. The *swords* of truth cut through the air and sharpen the mind. The pentacle, the *coin*, represents the wealth we've developed with our work and the health and material possessions we enjoy. And the *wand* represents the determination and strength of our spirit as we make our internal and external journey, providing fuel for our fire of passion to burn.

Obviously, there are other ways to interpret the symbolism, yet because culture is the art of our collective consciousness, the beauty and wonder of our paradigms is how they shift with different perspectives as well how they shift our perspectives. Were one to spend the time, the echoes of the idea that there are four distinct parts to our being could be traced through the four ventricles of our hearts and our four limbs, out into the four directions toward the four corners of the Earth, going well into the four seasons, understanding the four noble truths, to see the four faces of the Brahma, listening to the four gospels until the arrival of the four horsemen of the apocalypse throwing out four leaf clovers while preaching the four cardinal virtues.

I'm a former member of the 4-H Club (Sarasota County Ridin' Rednecks chapter), and I was born on the 4th of August, so I'm sort of fascinated by it. Suffice it to say that even the 4-H Club follows this paradigm. Following the 4-H motto, "To Make The Best Better", the 4-H pledge states, "I pledge my head to clearer thinking, my heart to greater loyalty, my hands to larger service, and my health to better living, for my club, my community, my country, and my world."

Through all of the synchronicity we may find in these various cultural paradigms, the essence of ABC^2 Economics is that it helps us align our hearts, minds, bodies, and spirits through the realization of our Artistry, Business, Citizenry, and Community, in celebration of the water, air, earth, and fire that allows us the opportunity to grow in harmony.

"In nature's economy," Vandana Shiva reminds us in *Earth Democracy: Justice, Sustainability, and Peace,* "the currency is not money, it is life." E.F. Schumacher echoed that sentiment when he said, "There is incredible generosity in the potentialities of Nature. We only have to discover how to utilize them."

In the early 20th century, American businesses started developing their business models with disposability in mind. The more products that were designed to be disposed of after use, the more opportunity there was to manufacture and sell more of those products. A century later, we are awash in disposable products, overwhelmed by garbage and pollution, and it seems that very few businesses produce products that last longer than a few uses.

We need a healthier version of materialism, one that actually appreciates material rather than only appreciating its disposability. As we've come to consider material as disposable, and lost touch with the elements of nature, viewing it as only a collection of resources to exploit, we have also often come to view humanity as disposable as well.

Ultimately, we not only need to develop practices that are not as environmentally destructive as the rampant consumerism we've been programmed to embrace, but to also learn from nature, which has been developing sustainably since long before our species even came into the picture and invented garbage. By fully realizing the value in all facets of creation, nature has never known of waste, has always sought equilibrium through diversity over domination, and throughout all of its various cycles and phases, continues to maintain balance through synergy. With as much as we think we know, we still have a lot to learn.

"In nature," says Charles Eisenstein in *Sacred Economics*, "headlong growth and all out competition are features of immature ecosystems, followed by complex interdependence, symbiosis, cooperation, and the cycling of resources. The next stage of human economy will parallel what we are beginning to understand about nature. It will call forth the gifts of each of us; it will emphasize cooperation over competition; it will encourage circulation over hoarding; and it will be cyclical, not linear. Money may not disappear anytime soon, but it will serve a diminished role even as it takes on more of the properties of the gift. The economy will shrink, and our lives will grow."

ABC² ECONOMICS

"The four characteristics of humanism are curiosity, a free mind, belief in good taste, and belief in the human race."
- E.M. Forster

Say what you will about economics, it is nothing if not idealistic. It is even imagined that there will come a time when the challenges it does pose are all worked out and no one will ever have to suffer from economic inequality or poverty again. The father of modern economics, John Maynard Keynes said, "the day is not far off when the economic problem will take the back seat where it belongs, and the arena of the heart and the head will be occupied or preoccupied, by our real problems - the problems of life and of human relations, of creation and behavior and religion."

We may still have a ways to go before we reach Keyes' ideal, but it may very well be that we are well on our way. And it is my hope that ABC² Economics can help us to do just that. But to prepare the arena of the heart and head, we need to know what we really want.

"True happiness," Aristotle wrote almost 2500 years ago, "flows from the possession of wisdom and virtue, and not from the possession of external goods. But a virtuous life must be equipped with external goals as instruments."

As Aristotle wrote centuries ago, and as pretty much every spiritual teacher and philosopher worth their salt has said since, material possessions are not the goal. Obviously, that wisdom stands in stark contrast to the current message of the Market Economy, where one of the fastest growing industries is storage space for all of our extraneous material possessions and other external goods. And one of the most difficult challenges to face nearly any human in this generation is to hear that wisdom over the din of the constant noise generated by the hucksters, salesmen, and celebrities of the marketplace, all trying to convince you that their goods will make you happy.

For those who wish to embrace the wisdom of the ages, we consciously make time to separate ourselves from the noise of the marketplace, enjoying moments of silence, empowering artistic flow, good company, and the virtues we truly seek rather than what the marketplace would have us pursue. We do not wait for the day when economic problems will take the back seat. We put them in the back seat. Then we can engage the arena of the heart and head, and address what is important to us rather than the fads and schemes of the marketplace.

For us to have a truly vibrant economy, we the people must do a better job of participating in it and taking control of it, and ironically, we must also let go of it and redirect our energy toward participating in the other aspects of our lives. That is, of course, a considerable challenge in this age of the 'attention economy' where the plethora of memes, articles, videos, and pictures all clamor for our cognizance. And it is especially difficult in a media landscape that showcases so many messages of anger, fear, grief, shame, and other forms of lower consciousness.

"Energy follows attention," C. Otto Scharmer says in *Leading from the Emerging Future: From Ego-System to Eco-System Economies*. "Wherever you place your attention, that is where the energy of the system will go. 'Energy follows attention' means that we need to shift our attention from what we are trying to avoid to what we want to bring into reality."

The human brain can only process 126 bits of information per second. If we hope to take control of our lives, we had better start paying more attention to which 126 bits are processed. Not only do we need to be more conscious of the media we consume, but also more considerate of the various levels of relationships we have with the world we inhabit.

"As individuals," Scharmer continues, "we must begin to pay attention to our attention (self-awareness); as teams, we must begin to converse about our conversations (dialogue); as enterprises, we must begin to organize our organizing (networks of networks: eco-systems); and as eco-systems, we must begin to coordinate our coordinating (systems of awareness-based collective action, or ABC)."

While this is certainly more complicated than merely continuing our existence as consumers while the Market Economy continues its drive toward domination, it does offer us those tangible "external goals" of which Aristotle spoke. And should we channel our effort and energy toward creating the world we want, we will have a much brighter and longer future than the marketplace would allow, one in which our true desires can come to light, rather than those that have been manufactured for us.

The basis of ABC^2 Economics is having the ability to channel energy toward our internal and external goals in order to develop a more vibrant overall economy for individuals and the collective. The New Economy, as outlined in ABC^2 Economics, offers a more holistic realization that the Market Economy does not exist in a vacuum between merely buyer and seller, but in a vast, interdependent network of Artists creating Businesses to establish a more resilient Citizenry in the development of a stronger Community.

By empowering people with a simple means of directing the flow of their economic energy, the intention is to develop the highest capacity for well-being as individuals and as a collective by more effectively realizing and sharing assets.

The ABC^2 Economics model builds on the four avenues through which people participate in society: the *Artistry* of life, the service of *Business*, engagement through *Citizenry*, and the development of *Community*. Obviously, each avenue reaches greater levels of complexity, and the paths do cross, yet these four activities account for the bulk of human behavior. This allows for a good starting point in understanding where we are, what we have to work with, and where we are going.

"This new generation of networked people understand they are living through a third industrial revolution," writes Paul Mason in *Postcapitalism: A Guide To Our Future*, "but they are coming to realize why it has stalled: with the credit system broken, capitalism cannot sustain the scale of automation that is possible, and the destruction of jobs implied by the new technologies. The economy is already producing and reproducing a networked lifestyle and consciousness, at odds with the hierarchies of capitalism. The appetite for radical economic change is clear. The next question is: what do we have to do to achieve it?"

It is my contention that we have to empower people to cultivate these four aspects of their lives: Artistry, Business, Citizenry, and Community. The digital innovations at our disposal makes it possible to have an open source, transparent economic system that will reflect our true wealth rather than usurp it. Since nearly 92% of the monetary supply is digital and has no physical existence, building on the blockchain technology that allows us to track the flow of each unit of currency, we also have the capacity to channel the flow and empower people to create our economy, rather than corporations and the politicians they employ.

Our life is our art. Regardless of whatever we may do within the confines of the space between birth and death, the one truth for every human being that has ever walked the planet is that their life is completely unique. Even for those who were born into less than fortunate circumstances, where choices may be very limited, each life still carries the opportunity to respond to circumstances and thus offers at least a glimmer of individual artistry.

Even in lives without much room for freedom of choice, in little ways, all through our days, people make little choices that carve out their individuality and help make their lives unique. The capacity with which we are able to decide the course of action for our lives and how we should live them is where the Artistry of life blossoms.

As they say, money cannot buy happiness, but it can buy freedom. And the freedom to make as much money as you want and spend as much money as you want on whatever you want is one of the greatest freedoms offered in a capitalistic society.

Financial freedom certainly does provide great power to those who are able to wield it. Yet as Uncle Ben told Peter Parker, with great power comes great responsibility. Unfortunately, the fine print in the capitalist brochure has historically alleviated responsibility from anything other than merely making money.

For 50 years, capitalists have rallied around the wisdom of Milton Friedman, whose idea that the only responsibility of a business is to increase profits for the stockholders was enough to win him the Nobel prize in economics. Yet five decades later, as corporations have stripped so much of the natural world in order to turn every last resource into money, even ardent capitalists are seeing the negative effects that such myopia can cause.

Beyond the isms of the past, people are seeking out better ways to both seize the power of their freedom as well as the responsibility of realizing ourselves as part of the bigger whole in order to create more vibrant art of our lives.

Online reality is the art of this generation. As such, each activity and every transaction has an artist behind it. Either through the product being sold or merely the pressing of keys to deliver information electronically, we are creating commercial presence. Thus, each of us that contributes to the digital economy is an online Artist.

Of course, the internet is largely a virtual representation of actual human society; whatever we do with our time and talent individually contributes to the art of life. As such, although I initially developed the idea of ABC^2 Economics with digital transactions in mind, it has the capacity to help us channel our energy in the physical world as well.

In the growing gig economy, many people play various roles. As we participate in the four facets of our being, as Artists, Businesses, Citizens, and Community members, we have the capacity to generate economic flow through multiple sources of income. Ultimately, all that we do, through

Business, Citizenry, and Community contributes to the **Artistry** of our lives. Finding ways to recompense, reward, and remunerate those who contribute to our lives is one of the primary tasks of ABC^2 Economics.

In order to share your art, from design and manufacturing to advertising and distribution, there are multiple people who contribute to bringing it to life and bringing it to market. Each of these people is a **Business** contributing to the Artistry of our lives and empowering us to share what we have to offer.

Historically, we have practiced a hierarchical means of **Citizenry** by paying taxes levied by governments. Since 1912, the US government has enforced an income tax philosophy that takes a chunk of each citizen's money before they can get to it in order to sustain government's own growth. However, the upsurge in freelancers, independent contractors, and smart contracts is making obsolete many unnecessary complexities throughout the Internal Revenue Service, and it offers us the opportunity to cultivate a more participatory and engaged democracy.

Our growing technological capacity offers us the opportunity to be more efficient. As blockchain technology and smart contracts become more prevalent, we eliminate the need for middlemen, which is the essence of government, and we can direct our individual energy directly toward causes we believe in in a way that is much more transparent than the lobbying and campaign contributions that currently corrupt our policies.

We are rapidly approaching a time when we will no longer need the governmental structures we now employ to manage our finances and resources because the dream of democracy will have manifested and the government will truly be of, by, and for the people... or at least closer than it is now.

Because all of our activity, our Artistry, Business, and Citizenry, has an impact on the world in at least some way, be it emotional, educational, environmental, or otherwise, we each contribute to the **Community** in order to support the greater whole. This is where we have historically created charitable organizations and NPOs to clean up our messes, fill in the gaps, and promote the things we love that don't fit as easily into the Market Economy. For those of who have a passion to see good done in the world and to do good ourselves, contributing to our community by helping the less fortunate, comforting the sick, educating the ignorant, and celebrating beauty is a very important part of our individual economic activity.

ABC^2 Economics may not be so idealistic as to put economics in the back seat, as Mr. Keynes hoped, but it does put people in the driver's seat, where they belong. By encouraging people to cultivate the four aspects of their lives and empowering them to channel their own economic energy, people will be able to drive the economy, and people will be able to finally drive the democracy. ABC^2 Economics seeks to offer a map through which to navigate this web of networks, teams, enterprises, and ecosystems we're creating.

Mapping out the Web

The internet is indeed a world wide web, and in order to make the most of it, and use it as an avenue for economic development, we need to make a map of how to get from where we are to where we want to be and how to channel our money so that it can get from where it is to where it needs to be. We need a WeBMaP.

In order to make ABC^2 Economics scalable, we need for people to be able to create a profile and select a primary identity as either an Artist, Business, Citizen, or Community member. Granted, any individual or organization could provide more than one offering or play more than one role, but each profile is given the ability to channel its economic flow as it sees fit.

For instance, as an Artist, I can create projects and collaborate with other Artists on developing new streams of revenue. Because I am a multi-faceted Artist, as I develop my profile, I can let potential collaborators know that I can serve as a song, script, copy, or poetry writer, rhythm guitarist, singer, actor, filmmaker, publisher, and other artistic roles that I may not have discovered yet. From there, I see what Businesses I can connect with to get people appreciating my art, then I make connections with the city, county, state, and country I happen to be a Citizen of at the time, and how I want to engage with the Community in creating a better world for all involved.

If a person of Business signs up, they are also going to be able to map out the products and services they provide in order to create multiple streams of revenue for themselves. Certainly, Artists can serve on projects as Businesses as well. In theory, so can organizations or individuals that also classify as a Citizen or Community member.

For any given project, a person could play different or multiple roles. As we play these roles, we map out the relationships and energy exchanges we experience along the way, allowing money to be the memory that it is, and encouraging it to flow the way that a currency should in a vibrant economy. Humans are, after all, multi-faceted beings. As we move beyond the corporate/industrial methodology of specialization, a lot of us are going to realize that we're a lot more talented and a lot more wealthy than we have been previously led to believe.

A WeBMaP will help us find our way.

How Does It Work?

Let's look at how a song can be developed to be an economic instrument through ABC^2 Economics.

Let's say that I produce a song and release it as a downloadable mp3, a digital product that can be repeatedly downloaded as a residual source of income with no extra labor for me other than telling people about it. Imagine if I could preset all of the variables for how the revenue from this product should be channeled and activate it to automatically transfer those funds to all who are involved.

Just as with most products, digital or otherwise, there is a lot of collaboration involved in a song. As the writer, I have rights to the song, and in producing that song, I am able to share ownership of the recordings with the other participating artists. This allows us to all prosper more greatly from the distribution of the song, while also contributing to the society in which the song will be most greatly appreciated.

In taking the song from words on paper to a produced recording, I start by recording the guitar track, then the lead vocals. Then the drummer comes in to record a track, followed by a bassist, a mandolin player, and a background vocalist. Finally, the sound mixer cleans it all up to make it sound smooth, and we have a finished song.

Because talent is not easily quantifiable, we consider each artist's investment in time. Evaluating the time that each Artist puts into a production allows us to properly allocate revenue to them when the production generates it.

Overall, not including the time to write the song, we've accumulated about a dozen hours of production time. The time that each artist has invested in the production of the song has been recorded, and we can log that into our Artist portfolio. Of course, now we need to consider the Business costs of getting the song to market. These include distribution, any advertising or marketing, touring and promotional costs, and whatever else it takes to get the song to the ears that want to hear it. So as the primary Artist, I make those connections with those who want to serve in those roles as affiliates.

In order to have a market in which people have enough stability and freedom to purchase musical and other artistic products, we need to have organizational structures that manage our collective resources and support an infrastructure that develops prosperity. This includes community organizations, schools, hospitals, city, county, state, and federal governments, and any other movements or institutions that contribute to a more engaged and effective Citizenry.

As the Artist of my life, I get to decide how much support I send to the organizations that contribute to supporting the world that allows me to make and share music. Basically, instead of the trickle-down income tax we've been serving for the last century, where the federal government absorbs the wealth and distributes it to states and municipalities, we instead empower people to invest more of their economic energy directly toward their local initiatives rather than have it hoarded and wasted by the beaurocracy of political theatre.

For instance, let's say that this particular song was set to channel 20% to the Sarasota Bay Estuary Program, 20% to the City of Sarasota, 20% to Sarasota County, 20% to the State of Florida, 10% to the United States, and 10% to the United Nations. That, to me, seems like a much more efficient use of that money than the entirety of it being squandered by the federal government and its addiction to antiquated antagonism. As we cultivate our true Citizenry, we invest in ways in which we can all have greater mobility to pursue our interests while also being caretakers of the planet upon which we interact.

And lastly, we recognize that beyond the mess we make as we create the art of our lives, the world is a pretty messy and dangerous place. In order to make the most of it and decrease the suffering we naturally experience and the suffering that we fabricate and manufacture, we recognize ourselves as part of a greater Community and work to lift one another up. This is how we evolve as a species, at least, it always has been before.

Art should reach beyond being a mere material product for mindless consumption and strive to help alter and uplift our consciousness and make us a better people. So the artists involved in a song or other product can decide to channel some of the energy it creates toward endeavors that help to mend and heal what our civilizational activity has broken in the first place. As the lead Artist of a project, I collaborate with others, and we decide how much revenue from each product will go to fund charitable endeavors and social profit organizations, meaning that some products may channel a small percentage of revenue to a number of different recipients or they could be used as fund raisers for one particular endeavor.

Let's say that these particular artists desire to use the song to help get water to the thirsty, food to the hungry, shelter to the homeless, and comfort for the sick and imprisoned. Let's say that the Community portfolio is equally divided so that a portion goes to charity:water; a portion goes to the All Faiths Food Bank; a portion goes into a land trust that purchases properties to offer Housing First opportunities; a portion goes toward a universal healthcare system to ensure that everyone gets the care they need; and a portion goes toward a rehabilitation system to replace the punish-for-profit prison industry that is currently destroying lives all over the country.

Once the project is set up with an ABC^2 Economics WeBMaP, each unit of currency it develops can be channelled toward these various portfolios to create the most efficient and effective means of financial distribution. For instance, let's say one mp3 download generates a unit of currency (and while it theoretically could be a yen, euro, bitcoin or time dollar, for the sake of simplicity, let's say it's a dollar). So, from the dollar that is generated by the sale of the song, let's say that seventy cents goes into the Artist portfolio, ten cents goes into the Business portfolio, ten cents goes into the Citizenry portfolio, and ten cents goes into the Community portfolio.

Of the seventy cents that goes into the Artist portfolio, half goes to the songwriter, and the rest is distributed to each of the contributing artists based on how much time each invested in the project. The ten cents that go into the Business portfolio are directed toward the affiliates who contribute toward bringing it to market and promoting it. The ten cents in the Citizenry portfolio are then channelled toward the city, county, state, and nation in which the song was produced, as well as any other endeavors that promote the greatest Citizenry. And the ten cents in the Community portfolio gets distributed to whichever social profit organizations or other charitable endeavors the Artists have selected.

While a single dollar may not seem like much of an economic generator, consider what it would generate if it sold a million copies. What if other artists were able to distribute their work in such a fashion, offering digital products, like photos, ringtones, podcasts, and ebooks, or even material products like framed prints, crafts, or pottery? What if filmmakers could use their collaborative prowess to tell stories and develop series that created residual streams of income for all of the artists involved, those who help promote it, the support of the world around them, and a positive change in the lives of others?

What if a million artists released their art into the digital marketplace with this sort of foundation, including the ability to change the percentages accordingly, and even to go deeper into each portfolio and engage more particularly with each endeavor? What if, instead of merely sending money to the federal government, citizens could decide how their money is spent and which initiatives it should support? What if, by realizing art as the instrument through which we can best manage money, humankind's most abiding artform, we can harness the power of a truer sense of democracy and make the older technologies of representatives and lobbyists obsolete?

Could this be the new mythology Joseph Campbell said we needed? What if we can use our art to change the world? That's the question of ABC^2 Economics.

Economy Beyond the Market

as we participate in business
we establish what we call a market
this is where we need to use our heads
we would be wise if we would hearken
the lessons that history has taught us
as we still continue to learn
what we're actually capable of
and how we should discern
where we put our attention
and how we find our purpose
how we use our time and talent
so that we can be of service
so we connect with like minds
who like what we have to offer
we look for win/win situations
so that both of us can prosper
where we have not used business well
is where it's a winner take all game
and history has proven
that we do better when we collaborate
much of the business we have going on right now
is making a pretty big mess
and we seem to have made it our business
to disdain and diminish
our true wealth for sheer busy-ness

for the last one hundred years
we've been the unwitting subjects
of psychological marketing
and advertising campaigns
by people who are totally obsessed
with ensuring that we're just good consumers
who keep making garbage
which makes them more money
and i know that it can get so much worse
and it is not going to be funny
when we've cut down all the rainforests
and sucked up all the oil
where we can no longer drink the water
or grow anything in the soil
and all that's left of humanity
is this ledger of our accounting
our silly belief that we control anything
with our most ubiquitous art form is astounding
but there is a chance we can use this tool
and it could bring greater benefit
if we can build on our nature to collaborate
and not always have to be so competitive
as we moved from industry to information
we became different types of consumers
and in the revolution we're spinning into
we've all become lifelong learners
now that so many tasks have been replaced
with artificial intelligence
let's promote humankind, empower education,
and invest in our own excellence
we are all the artists of our lives
we are the players on this stage
we color ourselves with emotions

we write a new beginning on every page
our species is the only one
that makes up all these stories
we constantly regale ourselves
with fables and allegories
we tell the stories of the gods who came before
to hammer everything out
and though we repeat these tales, way down deep
we also have our doubts
we're told the story of creation
and how all this was made for us
it does us little good to question it
so we just go along and trust
that the leaders who say they're our leaders
were placed there by some greater intelligence
but as we've come to realize
usually it's just dumb luck and happenstance
we tell stories about our differences
we've come up with races, classes, and factions
but our most amazing story is one we all share
it is the most incredible of our abstractions
this unit of value we all agree to
this symbol we have of our unity
there is no other story that we'd rather tell
than the one that we tell about money
yet the story we've told in the past
has been based on debt and based on scarcity
but we've gotten ourselves to the point
where we can now
move forward with much more creativity
the first thing we need to realize
is we've made it all up to this point

after slavery was abolished
money was a pretty good tool to exploit
the labor of the masses to serve the profits of a few
but with a growing class of billionaires
we should probably start anew
for the time being
let's just deal with what we've got
and see where the money has been dammed
and then let's get that back into the flow
and come up with a better plan
for anyone who has over a billion dollars
let's get the excess back into circulation
if you think you need more than that
to spend in this lifetime
you should be a mental patient
this obsession we have with this game
of seeing who can snatch up the most
it's kind of pathetic that we enable this behavior
just so they can boast
some may say
if we take away the right to be a billionaire
we'll lose the incentive
we'll lose drive and ambition
but i got to be honest, i'm okay with that
because i think we have an addiction
if selfishness is our highest virtue
and we honor nothing more than greed
then billionaires are perfectly fine
but personally i think we need
to honor people who don't need as much
people who just want to be
people who don't want to grind it or crush it
and don't always need to compete

people who want to make art and make friends
and who want to make every day count
people who don't need fortune and fame
because they realize that life is about
so much more than the things you buy and collect
it's the things that you give and let go
it's about the love you share and ideas you spread
and finding yourself in the flow
and i don't think the new economy
should be just about how much we can purchase
i think the goal we should all be striving for
is empowering one another to find purpose
so let's take the excess from the top
and put it where it's needed
and let billionaires be the leaders we need
by directing the flow to the people
what if we had an income
that was basic and universal
just so we can alleviate poverty
and ensure that every person
has enough to participate
in the economy we're building
and empower people to build a life
not just make a living
after all, all the money in the world
was made with resources to which we all have claim
so let's reset and redeal
with more understanding and wisdom
and let humanity start a new game
what if we just paid people
to be the artists of their lives?
you're paid to show up and just be yourself
but if you're inspired to apply

your attention and energy to other things
and you start to get ambitious
you learn whatever you need to know
so that you can go about your business
you find allies and build relationships
and network with other partners
you gain other opportunities
and your income starts to get larger
and for every project you work on
invest yourself to make a transaction that's digital
soon you find yourself with a number of endeavors
that produce an income that's residual
and you realize the more things that you do
the more that has to be done
and there's usually a bit of cleanup
after you've had your fun
so you direct some of the flow you've created
as the artist of your life
to those who empower you to do what you do
organizations and other allies
for healing the planet and lifting up others
you get to be responsible
by giving back and supporting the source
that makes all of this possible
for a while i've had this idea
about the technology of the future
but the essence of abc squared economics
is about more than just computers
it's a way to direct our energy
toward what we really are
we are spirits living in bodies
with fertile minds and wild hearts

and as we continue to realize
the tools that are available
to help us create the lives we envision
there is so much of which we are capable
life is the gift that keeps on giving
to continue to be the artist of your life
find others to serve and you will find business
be part of the greater community
and participate as a citizen
whatever role you’re playing
always give your best performance
and soon enough you'll find yourself trading
in abc squared economics

Minding the Gap

**"We're trying to democratise financial services,
to ensure that management and movement of money
is a right for all citizens, not the privilege of the affluent."
- Dan Schulman, President and CEO, PayPal**

In 2011, I challenged myself to live for a year without using money. I did pretty well considering the daunting challenge of living in a society based on money while not trying to use it, but it wasn't a perfectly executed endeavor. Nevertheless, it did give me some time to think about how I'd used money in the past, and how I felt it should be used in the future.

When I finally started using money again, I opened five different bank accounts. I have an Artistry account, a Business account, a Citizenry account, a Community account, and a savings account.

As an Artist, I have multiple streams of income, and they are all deposited into my Artistry account. Currently, when I receive a payment, I manually transfer 10% into my Business account, my Community account, and my savings account. I also transfer 40% into my Citizenry account.

My Business account is set up with automatic payments for my cell phone, data storage and cloud services, website fees, and other regularly scheduled costs that pertain to my doing business. I also use this account to pay for anything that will help me grow my business, including educational experiences, equipment, and, of course, marketing.

I've heard that a person's housing costs should be no more than 30% of their income, so 30% of my income goes toward paying my rent. Theoretically, the other 10% of the 40% of my income I put toward Citizenry will go toward supporting the governments whose services I enjoy. However, realistically, I haven't actually made all that much money since I started using it again, so so far it's been sufficient for me to know that at least a portion of my rent is going toward property taxes. I do imagine that one day this entire 30 or 40% could be used to make sure I have housing that meets my needs, and a government that helps meet everyone's needs, but it could be that just 10% is sufficient for a better functioning government.

With my Community account, I have been able to support various charitable and environmental organizations and GoFundMe campaigns, help two friends pay rent when they were unemployed, help another friend fix her broken van, and basically help people when they needed it. As I become more successful as an artist, and increase the streams of revenue as well as the volume, this account will be used to support more charitable organizations and help more people.

Currently, I do all of this manually. However, my hope is to collaborate with designers who can help make this payment system automatic and scalable. What if we were to empower every American to channel their money in a similar manner? What if we were to empower everyone in the world to do it?

A major peer-reviewed study by Nobel Prize-winning economist Angus Deaton and his colleague Daniel Kahneman at the Center for Health and Well-Being at Princeton University made a case for the cost of happiness. The study showed that after people made more than 75,000$ a year, extra money did not seem to increase their enjoyment of day-to-day experiences. That said, let's examine what would happen if I were to receive a 75,000$ salary under ABC^2 Economics.

If I manage to achieve a state in which I make 75,000$ in a year, using ABC^2 Economics with only 10% toward each account, I could channel 7500$ toward my business and marketing expenses, 7500$ to my governmental and environmental protection organizations, 7500$ to charitable endeavors, and 52,500$ toward creating the art of my life. Or I could also adjust the flow of the channels to see economic growth expand as I would like to see it expand.

Perhaps I would like to see my business opportunities flourish more. I could channel a greater percentage in that direction so that I would have 10,000$ or 20,000$ go toward those expenses and only channel 50,000$ or 40,000$ into my Artistry account. Or maybe I'd like to give more to charity and increase my giving from 10% of my economic energy to 20% or 50%.

However any of us may decide to channel our financial flow, if we're truly going to create a democratic society, it should be up to us as to what initiatives get our support. By empowering people with the ability to choose how to support the world we live in, we will no longer have to rely on people who don't actually have the wherewithal to make decisions on our behalf and usually make decisions based on what they think will make more money for people who just can't get enough of it. We will be able to create a stronger economy by developing a healthy economic flow instead of just making certain bank accounts grow.

In establishing an economy that flows, rather than one based on amassing fortune, we must start by realizing that it must reach the entirety of the community. Ultimately, the community is the body of the people and money is the blood. Just as stopping the flow of blood to any organ results in disease and decay, so does the hoarding of money and blocking its flow to the entirety of the community reap disease and decay in humanity.

It is rather interesting that Andrew Yang's idea for Universal Basic Income is to give every American 1000$ a month. When you consider that there is currenly 90 trillion dollars' worth of money that humanity has created, and if we were to evenly distribute it to all 7.5 billion of us, we would each get about 12,000$, which could certainly be distributed as 1,000$ a month. Just imagine what a year that would be, were we to completely redistribute the collective currencies we've created so that everyone on the planet had 1,000$ a month to spend.

Granted, it is highly unlikely that that sort of financial redistribution is going to happen, but I think it's an incredible notion to consider, and I may just be inspired to at least write a fictional account of it someday. However, as we do come to realize that the legal fiction of money is going to need another rewrite, we must consider what sort of story we want to tell. Just imagine that we do figure out a way to allow our currency to flow effectively, and the stability I am offered empowers me to make more of my other talents, and I am eventually able to acheive my goal of figurative happiness by making 75,000$ a year.

If I channel 10% of my financial flow toward governmental and environmental protection organizations to represent my Citizenry, I should have some choice on what that money goes toward rather than relying on the trickle down method, whereby the federal government consumes more than its fair share, leaving too little for local governments and initiatives. Of the 7500$ I invest in my Citizenry, I should be able to channel 500$ into my neighborhood, 2000$ into my city, 2000$ to my county, 1500$ to my state, 1000$ to my country, and 500$ to the United Nations.

That, to me, seems like it would be a far more effective use of that money than if the federal government were to just take it all and spend it on unnecessary administration, bureaucracy, and the ridiculous wastefulness of antiquated partisanship and juvenile competition.

Now, imagine that every American household were to channel their revenue in such a way. What if we exempted the 19% of Americans who were under the poverty line, but empowered Americans that made between 25,000$ and 200,000$ a year to channel 10% of their income toward more effective citizenry? Without even accounting for the 8.5% who make more than 200,000$, not even accounting for any millionaires or billionaires, we could still generate well over 6 trillion dollars.

That's a lot more than the 3.86 trillion dollars the US government expects to take from its people this year, and just imagine how much more effectively it could be spent if we focused on local initiatives first rather than engaging the spectator sport of national politics. Basically, the idea behind ABC^2 Economics is about how we take our power back and create a more efficient and effective method of celebrating this thing called life.

My hope is that the heart behind this idea starts to direct the flow and others can see the vision. To actually make it work and make it scalable, we're going to need a lot of minds that know a lot more about coding than I do. And, or course, all of these transactions and algorithmic activity is going to increase our energy use, but it could also help us lessen some of the current usage that is really sucking us dry.

Ultimately, whether or not ABC^2 Economics could actually work as a system, or whether or not whatever other ideology promises to save us will work, will be up to the users. If we open ourselves up to the economy of *oikonomia*, we will recognize that every little thing we do with the 1,440 minutes of time we're given in each of the 365 days we're afforded each year comprised of 8,765 hours of emotions, expressions, relations, libations, creations, collaborations, locations, negotiations, sensations, temptations, expectations, operations, fluctuations, and regulations that contribute to the world we all share. Regardless of the technologies we engage to develop our collective economy, how well it meets our individual needs starts with the individual.

The essence of ABC^2 Economics is personal as well as collective. It's about empowering people to make their own decisions instead of enabling the financial powers that be to continue making the short-sighted decisions that are currently having such adverse effects on us. It's about having some hope in humanity.

Today

today is a new day
as we watch tomorrow fade away
the world we knew has been led astray
down the wrong road
we don't know which way to go

as we try to find our balance
faith has become a challenge
the only thing that we can manage
is how we cope
and keep our hope

now, we feel all alone
cut off from all that we've known
the world is out of control
beyond our limit
what day is it?

we get
to use this as a reset
if only we could pardon debt
and just let
ourselves be
what we can be

gotta move past where we disagree
dogma is not a skeleton key
we're all branches of the same tree
there is no one way
we all gotta be the change

to be free, we must set free
give liberty to everybody
live each day in jubilee
learn to forgive
so we can live

what we gotta do is let go
of the life that we've known
and open up to the flow
to find a better way

we can follow
a path that will feed our soul
where we want to see growth
namaste is how we pray

a new beginning begins every day
so let it start now
make a difference, be the better way
any way how
i'm the only change that i can make today

about the author

Steve McAllister has long considered himself a renaissance man, largely due to the fact that he wants to see a renaissance happen in the world. After hitchhiking across the country in 2001 and challenging himself to live for a year without money in 2011, his experiences have birthed a variety of poetry and songs, and 2021 finds him wanting to travel the country by motorcycle to share them. His previous one person shows include *The Cowboy Cabaret*, *Will Rogers Revived*, and *Seamus O'Day and the Irish Way*, and his books include *The Rucksack Letters*, *How To Survive An Estralarian Mind Meld*, *Money, Sex, Power & Faith; Questioning The Building Blocks of* Civilization, and *Cowboy Up: The Poetry Of The Cowboy Cabaret*. He has also released a CD of original songs titled *Be Here Now*, and another is in production.

www.stevemc.xyz
@SteveMcAlphabet

www.ingramcontent.com/pod-product-compliance
Lightning Source LLC
LaVergne TN
LVHW020635100826
845148LV00012B/2190

* 9 7 8 1 7 3 4 6 9 1 0 5 4 *